Yes You Can!

Everything You Need From A to Z to Influence Others to Take Action

Stacey Hanke & Mary Steinberg

authorHOUSE®

AuthorHouse™
1663 Liberty Drive, Suite 200
Bloomington, IN 47403
www.authorhouse.com
Phone: 1-800-839-8640

First published by AuthorHouse   9/2/2008

ISBN: 978-1-4389-0443-6 (sc)

Library of Congress Control Number: 2008906740

Printed in the United States of America
Bloomington, Indiana

This book is printed on acid-free paper.

Contents

Introduction

"Change your thoughts and you change your world."

– Norman Vincent Peale

IS THIS BOOK FOR YOU?

We know you can relate to what Norman Vincent Peale said. We also know you can have influence on others. If we are correct, this book is for you.

It is for you if you believe professionals are always in school. You know who you are. You are one who understands there is always something more when it comes to your development.

It is for you if you are one who knows what your strengths and weaknesses are–you are looking for practical techniques to eliminate your weaknesses and to enhance your strengths.

It is for you if you are one who is not aware of your strengths and weaknesses. When you think about people who you consider the best communicators, you never think of yourself. Following the suggestions in this book will change your way of thinking.

CHOICES, CHOICES, CHOICES

Communication is often a succession of choices you make to influence others to take action. The choices you make will influence the level of your success. Those choices include the words you say, the tone of voice you use, the way you stand and much more.

You can probably point to some success in your life when you were at your best at influencing others. Not just good or adequate, but at your best. If someone had been recording you with a stop-action camera and a mind-reading device, you would know exactly what you did, what you said, what you thought (yes, even thoughts play a role). If you re-created all of this in subsequent communications, you could be at your best over and over again. Some of what you did will be obvious. For instance, you knew how to motivate a particular audience by offering benefits that were specific to their interests. Most likely there will be some things that played a part in your success you may not be aware of.

You probably do not think to yourself, "Wow, I sure was authentic. No wonder I got the response I wanted." Being authentic does have an impact in getting the response you want from others. This book is about digging deeper and providing everything you need to know from **A** to **Z** to reach that pinnacle of success over and over again.

WHAT IS THIS BOOK'S FOCUS?

The primary focus of **Yes You Can!** is face-to-face communication. Why? It seems to be on the verge of becoming a lost art. Who does not know someone who has sent a text message to the person in the next cubicle asking the person to do something? What a shame, as face-to-face is the most effective way to communicate when you want to influence someone to take action.

The face-to-face situations we address are the meetings you hold, the presentations you give to groups, the face-to-face conversations you have, and any others when you are asking people to take action. What you will find is most of what you will read here will apply to any of those situations. If there is something specific to a particular situation, we will make that distinction.

How is this book designed?

We provide practical ideas from **A** to **Z**. We group the ideas by chapters that represent each letter of the alphabet. The ideas within each chapter are not always in alphabetical order but in the order that provides the best flow for the concepts. We recommend you read the **A's** first, as the concepts of **Attitude, Authenticity** and **Audience** are the foundation for the remainder of the book. After that, skip around when you want. If you are using PowerPoint next week in a presentation, for example, go to the **Visual Aids** section to get tips for being at your best when you use it. The table of contents shows you what is covered under each letter.

We have identified some of the ideas as essential for any face-to-face interaction. They will be noted by the use of the symbol **!**. The essential ideas are just that–essential to your ability to be at your best. If you adopt only a few of these essentials, you can still be successful, but not at your very best. The major league baseball pitcher who pitches a shutout is pretty darn good, but he would relish that no-hitter even more. Maybe you are the one who won this year's award for top sales performer. When you compare your numbers to last year's and see they are lower, you know you were not at your best.

Throughout this book you will have opportunities to develop your own set of best practices. We invite you to use a pen or pencil as you read this book. Highlight, underline, circle or do anything you need to mark sections you find useful. Throughout the book we will offer our own suggestions for practicing techniques under the heading of **Yes You Can!** following each chapter. We invite you to add your own ideas. This book will work for you not because of the ideas we give you but because of what you do with them. Ideas do not change a thing; it is only the actions you take around them that are important.

OUR WRITING STYLE

We have worked with thousands of people and have been fortunate to have seen what helps people be at their best when communicating. We will share many of our experiences. We share these experiences because of the value these individuals have brought to us and others. Some of these experiences occurred as we worked together, others occurred to us as we worked individually with others, but we present them as if they all happened to both of us because our experiences are so similar.

We work with groups in workshops and with individuals in one-to-one consultations. We use digital cameras to record them as they practice communication techniques. We play back the disks as a review tool. Many of our comments are as a result of our observations from this technique.

Our style is conversational. We focus on the practical. We want you to be able to take action immediately.

We encourage you to have real conversations with us after you finish the book. We want to hear about your successful face-to-face communication situations. You can share your stories at www. yesyoucanbook.com.

READY?

There is nothing more to say than to ask you to start with the **A**'s.

Attitude !

"If you go on stage with the wrong attitude or the performance is off, you can lose an audience in the first minute. The first minute is crucial."

– Allan Carr, film producer

The first minute of any type of face-to-face communication is crucial. Your attitude is the foundation for success. After you read this section, ask yourself whether you need to make an attitude adjustment at times.

We frequently hear individuals say about communication situations, "I just want to get through this" or "Once I get past the first minute, I feel comfortable." With these attitudes, what do you think the impact is on their audiences? When someone "just wants to get through it," there is a good chance the audience is thinking the same thing.

Have you ever said or thought similar things? When you tell yourself you need a minute to feel comfortable, you may as well tell your audience not to listen for the first minute. If this is your attitude, you may be better off not delivering the message at all. Make an attitude adjustment. Think instead about the valuable information you are going to share with your audience.

There are individuals who are 100 percent convinced the topics they present are boring. They are so convinced of this they often state it out loud. Have you done this? How do you think your message will come across with that attitude? When you feel this way and state it, it is hard to be anything but boring. As others have said, there are no boring topics, only boring speakers. An attitude adjustment is needed.

Another sign you need an attitude adjustment is if you fall into this trap: "I am nervous speaking in front of my peers." Once again you have convinced yourself how you will feel before you say a word. Instead you should be thinking the people listening to you want to hear what you have to say.

Attitude affects your choice of words and your thoughts. If you start with a negative attitude, your thoughts, feelings and words can quickly turn against you and cause a physical impact. The dry mouth begins, followed by sweaty palms, rushed speech, poor eye contact, and so on and so forth. Wow! Why make your job as a communicator harder than it needs to be?

Attitude is catching. We mirror off of one another. Think of how you react when you hear people speak. If they are nervous, how does that make you feel? If someone is obviously rushing to get through something, is it possible for you to be engaged?

Your attitude influences not only how you begin but also how you continue. If you start with a negative attitude, it is hard to change it and recover. Even if you can, you may have already lost your audience.

Here is the good news. You do not have to rely on anyone else to adjust your attitude. You have complete control. We trust you see attitude is essential to your success. Authenticity is also.

AUTHENTICITY !

Authenticity can be defined as the state of being genuine. To be the best communicator you can be, it is important to be genuine and allow others to see this. Being the best is about being genuine, not about being perfect.

We were asked to meet with a vice president of an organization who wanted to change the way the company's sales representatives delivered messages about its products. This was going to be a major change for most of them. At our initial meeting with him and his staff, he ran into the room, rattled off a number of items, did not ask for any comments, and ran out. His staff turned to us and said they hoped we understood what he wanted because they were unsure. We had a second meeting with the same group of people that started off the same way. This time, as he got up to run out, we quickly said, "Can you give us an example of the type of message you would like to hear?"

He sat down and said, "I feel overwhelmed with all that needs to be done. Do you think what I am asking for is even possible?" Bingo! We finally saw the real person. What was interesting is even though he was voicing how overwhelmed he felt, it was the first time we saw him relax. It was at that point we had real conversations about what was necessary to influence the change he was looking for.

Being authentic involves trusting yourself and trusting your audience. Trust what your audience wants is the real you. It is easier for them to relate to your message if they can relate to you.

Why is this difficult to do? Why did he not tell us from the beginning he was overwhelmed? Was it because he did not know us very well? Was it because he thought his title prevented him from thinking he could ask for help? Or, was this his standard way of operating? Whatever the reason, lack of authenticity made it difficult for us as his audience to take the action he wanted us to take.

This really goes back to what we presented under **Attitude**. In this case, if his initial attitude in our first meeting had been "I need some help on this project," he could have saved all of us some anxiety.

The feedback we love getting the most is about our authenticity. When we hear people say, "You are so genuine" it means we are at our very best. We realize there are steps we take to ensure authenticity is there. You can take these steps also. We share some under the **Yes You Can!** section at the end of this chapter.

AUDIENCE !

Having the right attitude and being authentic is taking care of you. Now it is time to think about your audience.

Knowing your audience helps you tailor the message in a way that increases your success at influencing the action you want them to take. The more you know about your audience, the better. Ask yourself the following questions about your audience.

- Who are they?
- What do they know about your subject?
- What do they need to know about your subject?
- What is their attitude towards your subject? And you?
- What is the attitude you would like them to have?
- What are their expectations?
- What action do you want them to take?
- What is in it for them when they take the action you are recommending?
- Is this the best time to meet with your audience?
- Is face-to-face the best way to communicate this message?

Thinking of who your audience is and what they need might seem obvious, but most people tend to bypass this step. How will you know this information? Some of the answers you will already have from your past experiences. In other situations you will need to ask your contact person, others who have had experience working with this audience or the audience itself when you meet with them.

We have an example of doing that. We work with pharmaceutical sales representatives at times. They are almost always gregarious, expressive and ready to be pushed hard. We know this from the moment they walk into the room because of the energy that surrounds them. They want to be in the room with us.

On one occasion we were surprised when a group from one of the pharmaceutical companies walked into the room. They were quiet, avoided eye contact and gave us the impression they would rather be at the dentist having a root canal than be with us.

Remember the first thing we discussed in this book was attitude. Why did we think they did not want to be there? We really had no idea, because they did not tell us this. We needed to stop thinking about our attitude about them and find out what was the real deal.

The first thing you need to know about your audience is: Who are they? So we asked this group who they were: "What department are we working with today?" They responded they were from the accounting department. When we realized we were working with a different group than in the past, we knew we needed to find out more about them.

Before we continued, we asked, "What do you know about our subject? What information would benefit you? What are your expectations?" This gave us enough information to make sure our message was tailored to them. We adjusted our attitude. We stopped thinking they did not want to be there and started thinking instead of what value we could add to their day.

Even though you come prepared with an A to Z plan, you always need to know there are times when it is necessary to adapt. The best communicators are people who can change their message on the spot to meet their audiences' needs and expectations.

The feedback we received on our performance from the accounting staff was as positive as the feedback we had received from pharmaceutical representatives. We asked this group to develop an action plan at the end of the session. Every participant had tangible action steps as a result of our message. We had influenced them to take action. When you take into consideration what your audience needs to hear, action is the result.

It is often said people remember things best when presented in groups of three. **Attitude**, **Authenticity** and **Audience** are the three most essential items in this book. You will see every other idea has some tie to at least one of these concepts.

Yes You Can!

ATTITUDE !

- Ask yourself if there are times you need an attitude adjustment. For example, if your attitude before a presentation is "I just want to get through this," how can you adjust your attitude? One way is to approach the presentation with a different perspective. "I want to make sure I give my audience what they need." "I am fortunate to have this opportunity because of what it could result in." "What is the worst thing that could happen?"

- Learn to take a compliment. Recognize most people are their own worst critics. If you doubt that, look at the following results of an experiment we conducted recently. We decided to compliment everyone we had contact with over a one-week period. The compliments had to be genuine.

  Only 35 percent simply said "thank you." Everyone else seemed to have a need to tell us why we were wrong. If we complimented peoples' outfits, they would tell us how old the outfits were. If we complimented peoples' hairstyles, they would tell us they were past due for a haircut. If we complimented peoples' knowledge about something, they would tell us what they did not know.

  The next time you receive a compliment, feel good about it, accept it as honest and refuse to negate it.

- Remember this important reality: *"They won't remember most of what you say; they will remember how you make them feel."* – Chris Gardner, motivational speaker.

- Stop thinking about yourself. Think about your audience and what they need from you.

AUTHENTICITY !

- Speak from the heart. When the vice president we mentioned did so, we were able to do what he was asking of us.

- Being authentic is another opportunity to adjust your attitude, if necessary. Do not think you have to be perfect. Start thinking you have to be yourself. That is what your audience wants.

- Be yourself at all times. We often hear people say they are different people at home than they are at work. Really? So which persona is the false one? You know we are not talking about what you wear at home as opposed to what you wear at work. We are talking about your values.

AUDIENCE !

- At the very least, start asking yourself the questions we presented earlier under **Audience**.

- Get into the habit of verifying at least one thing you think you know about your audience when you meet. This lets your audience know you have thought about them. It also lets you know if you need to make any changes based on inaccurate information.

Add any other ideas you have for yourself

_____

_____

_____

_____

_____

_____

Beginnings

How you begin a face-to-face conversation, a meeting or a presentation can have an impact on the outcome. Earlier under **Attitude**, we stated people often tell us, "Once I get past the first minute, I feel comfortable." Many people also tell us they just do not know how to begin.

What are some effective ways to begin that will help you get off on the right foot?

Meetings

We have attended many meetings when the following question is asked, "Has everyone received a copy of the agenda? Yes? Okay, let's get started." Started usually means diving right into the first item.

Having received an agenda is not the same thing as understanding the agenda. When you bring people together for a meeting, there is an expectation something will be accomplished.

After asking if everyone has received the agenda, review the goals and expectations. Let the people attending know what you need from them to have a successful meeting. Answer any immediate questions people have about the agenda. Then start with the first item.

Face-to-face conversations

Has the following ever happened to you? Someone you know comes up to you and immediately tells you what he or she needs without saying hello? The first thing you say is, "Whatever happened to hello?" Usually the person nervously laughs, apologizes, says hello and continues to talk at you. You may be listening to the person half-heartedly because there may still be a part of you that is thinking about the initial lack of acknowledgment.

All of us have probably been guilty of this at one time. There is an easy fix for this faux pas. When you approach someone you need to speak to about an action you want the person to take, a simple hello is usually all that is needed to get a conversation started. This does not mean to quickly say something that sounds like "Hello Ron I need you to complete the report by ..."

After you say hello, stop talking to let the other person take this in before you say anything else. This simple acknowledgment is an invitation to the other person to have a conversation with you. You will be more successful in getting what you want if it involves a conversation rather than a directive.

PRESENTATIONS

We cannot even tell you how many presentations we have attended that began with someone saying something that sounds like this: "Hello, my name is Debra and I am here today to talk to you about ..." We are sure you have heard (and maybe even said) the same. Does this ever grab your attention? Chances are you know her name is Debra, you know it is today, and you know what she is going to talk about because it is on the agenda.

A much better way to begin is to connect with your audience, ask them for their immediate interaction and tell them what is in it for them if they take action.

CONNECTING

You will be much more successful in getting what you want if you make an immediate connection with your audience. Remember to consider who your audience is. What would be of interest to them? Is it a story they can relate to? Have you read or heard a pertinent quote? Is there a reference you have just read in a newspaper or business journal that is pertinent to their needs? Is there a question you can ask them that will immediately get them thinking?

ASKING FOR INTERACTION

After you make that connection, tell them what you would like them to do while they are listening to you. Do you want them to consider how the information you are presenting is applicable to their circumstances? Do you want them to keep an open mind or express any reservations? This is your time to get your audience involved rather than telling them you are there today to talk to them about something.

TELLING THEM WHAT IS IN IT FOR THEM

What are the benefits to your audience if they do what you ask? Benefits are so important to motivating people we have given them their own separate section.

BENEFITS

Someone once told us she would always say no to kids that sold chocolate candies for their schools, churches or baseball teams because she knew she would eat too much if she bought anything. One day she saw a young boy who was selling chocolate bars. As she walked by him ready to say no, he said "You look like you have a sweet tooth." She turned around and bought three chocolate bars. She told us he was the first kid who had ever thought about what was in it for her.

This young man should go into sales. Have there been times when you said no more than once to someone trying to sell you something, then finally said yes? More than likely it is because they finally thought about you and the benefits for you.

One of the most important ways to motivate others to do what you are asking of them is to provide benefits. These benefits should be specific to your audience. Knowing your audience is the key to knowing what benefits are important to them. Saving time, receiving a monetary reward or getting promoted are safe bets if the actions they are taking warrant such benefits. Do not always play it safe. Use relevant information you may have about your audience to determine what else would motivate them.

Some of the actions you ask others to take are ones that are smaller in the grand scale of actions. They may not warrant increased pay, but they do warrant some acknowledgment of appreciation. Acknowledging others is significant to your ability to influence others to act.

We would like to go back to Debra. She is the one we mentioned under the presentations section of **Beginnings**. If she uses our suggestions under **Beginnings** and **Benefits**, a typical beginning might sound like this:

"I read an article in this morning's newspaper that said the most successful people are those who encourage others to think. I am asking you to practice pausing when you speak. You will see it gives you time to put thoughts to your words. It also allows others to take the time needed to think about what you have said."

We feel this is so much stronger than "Hello, my name is Debra and I am here today to talk to you about …"

Your words can help you connect to your audience. You want to be sure your body language does not interfere with your connection.

BODY LANGUAGE !

Over the years, we have asked thousands of people how they wanted to be perceived by others when they communicate. Confident, engaging, interesting, knowledgeable and trustworthy are some of the answers we hear most often. What would you tell us?

No matter what situation you find yourself in when you communicate, we assume you will not begin by telling your audience you are confident, engaging, interesting, knowledgeable or trustworthy. They do not have to hear you say it. Your body language will say it for you.

Attitude can have an impact on your body language. Do not just say you want to be confident. Believe it. Then show it. Actions speak louder than words. If you want to be perceived as confident, stand tall. If you want to be perceived as engaging, smile. If you want to be interesting, use gestures to paint a picture for your audience.

The reverse is also true. Your body language can have an impact on your attitude. If you are sitting in a chair right now, slouch down into it. How do you feel? We are going to guess it is not engaging.

Your body language can have a major impact on others' perceptions of you. Have you ever had anyone ask you if something was wrong and you asked "Why would you ask that?" The person tells you it is because you look serious, angry or disengaged. This comment surprises you because you are really happy to see this person. Then you are told you have your arms folded across your chest, you are frowning and you keep looking into the distance. Your attitude is you are really happy to see this person but your body language is saying to the person, "I wish you were not here." You may be sabotaging your message without even realizing it.

When your body language is inconsistent with your message it can confuse your audience. They may begin to question your intent. The impact body language has on your ability to be at your best in influencing others is critical.

Yes You Can!

BEGINNINGS

- Begin your next meeting, face-to-face conversation or presentation in a way that is different from the way you usually begin. Try at least one of the methods we suggested.

- Open with a question geared to your audience.

- Open with a story or quote that is of interest to your audience.

- Read your city's Sunday paper the weekend of your next important interaction. What current story would be of interest to your audience? Be creative.

BENEFITS

- Before you deliver your message make sure the benefits are for your audience – not for the organization, not for the world in general and not for you.

- Be careful of the words you use when you state the benefits for your audience. If you are asking your audience to implement a new procedure because the benefit will make them more productive, they may interpret this as, "Great, now I have more work to do." Instead you may tell them, "When you implement this new procedure it will make your life easier."

BODY LANGUAGE !

- Read the following sections of this book to get practical suggestions on how to leave your audience with the perception you want to convey.

  Posture, Movement, Gestures, Facial Expressions and Eyes

- Practice, practice, practice what you have read.

Add any other ideas you have for yourself

_____

_____

_____

_____

_____

_____

CHANGE

How do you react to change? We knew someone whose constant refrain to almost anything he was asked to do differently was "I am too old to change." He even said that when we asked him to try gesturing while talking rather than standing with his hands constantly in his pockets. This man was in his mid-fifties. We finally asked him how old he was when he first said he was too old to change. He laughed but did not say anything.

The next day he told us he thought about what we had asked him. He said he realized it was the current excuse he used for resisting change. He felt it was one excuse most people would accept because of his age. He realized he had used other excuses at other times in his life when he felt uncomfortable about trying something new. He told us he was now willing to try some gestures. Most importantly, he decided he was not going to say he was too old to change anymore.

This book helps you be at your best when you influence others to take action. Asking others to take action often means you are asking others to change in some way. How can you ask and expect others to change if you are not willing to change when necessary?

We began this book with the Norman Vincent Peale quote stating if you change your thoughts, you can change the world. The more willing you are to take a look at yourself and how you react to change can help you be a role model for others.

CONFIDENCE !

"I was always looking outside of myself for strength and confidence, but it comes from within."

– Anna Freud

We mentioned under **Body Language** we often ask people how they wanted to be perceived when they communicate to others. Confident is the most frequent answer we get.

If you want others to perceive you as confident, you should know already where you need to begin. It is with yourself, just like Anna Freud said. What do you need to do? First, start with **Attitude** and **Authenticity**. Second, know your **Audience**.

There are many other things that can help. Stand or sit tall. Look at people when you talk. We often hear people say they are more confident when they have time to prepare before a meeting, a face-to-face conversation or a presentation. Be prepared. It is going to show. You will feel confident and others will see that.

When you are truly confident, you can ask for others' opinions even knowing they may be different from your own. It is easier to stand your ground when you need to. It is easier to say you are wrong when someone else gives you information that changes your way of thinking.

Having confidence lets you realize it is rarely necessary to have 100 percent of the answers to every question you receive. When you say "I will get back to you" with confidence, the person asking the question will believe you.

When you are confident with your message, others will see it and hear it. They will feel more confident in taking the action you have asked them to take. A key factor to ensuring this shared feeling of confidence is to be consistent.

CONSISTENCY !

A very simple definition of consistency is that it is the absence of contradictions. In most communication classes, there is great emphasis on the importance of avoiding inconsistent messages by paying attention to body language and voice. When you say you are happy to be somewhere, your facial expressions and vocal characteristics should align with your words. We address this in the sections under **Body Language, Inflection** and **Vocal Projection.**

We want to also highlight the importance of consistency within the message itself. We once observed a senior manager conducting a meeting about an upcoming merger. At the beginning of the meeting, he stated to everyone how excited he was about the merger because of the great opportunities it provided to everyone. As people were getting ready to take a break, he leaned back in his chair and mumbled to the person on his right, "I can't believe we are doing this again. Who knows what is going to happen?" At that very moment, we saw the dynamics in the room change. Someone who overheard the comment asked what he meant. Someone else asked if he thought jobs were at risk. His demeanor also changed. He became defensive.

We know there are things you cannot say to people. Again, know who your audience is and what you can say. Be consistent with that message. That does not mean the message is always the same. If circumstances change, the message may change. Until that happens, the message needs to be consistent.

Yes You Can!

CHANGE

- Make a list of the changes you are encountering now. Your list should include changes you have chosen, changes imposed on you, changes you look forward to, changes you have some anxiety about and so on.

_____

_____

_____

_____

_____

_____

_____

_____

- Which change listed above presents the most difficult challenge for you?

_____

_____

_____

_____

_____

- How are you reacting to this change?

_____

_____

_____

_____

_____

- What do you need to do differently?

_____

_____

_____

_____

_____

CONFIDENCE !

- Are you feeling confident about an upcoming face-to-face interaction? If so, based on what you have read so far, will your audience perceive you as confident?

If not, what do you need to do for this to happen?

- Do you need to change your attitude?
- Do you need to know more about your audience?
- Do you need to change any habits with your body language?
- Anything else?

CONSISTENCY !

- When you have a difficult message or you are not confident with the message, do you tend to sugarcoat it?

  If so, practice stating your message with a trusted colleague in a way that is consistent with the reality of the message and appropriate for your audience.

Add any other ideas you have for yourself

_____

_____

_____

_____

_____

_____

Disparity

Fold your arms in front of your chest. Look at which arm is on top. Shake your arms out and fold them again with the opposite arm on top. How does this feel? If you are like everyone else we have asked to do this, you probably feel uncomfortable. We guarantee no one would know this but you.

This incongruity between how you feel and how you appear to others is known as disparity. This is a critical concept to understand. The importance of it goes well beyond our asking you to fold your arms to experience a bit of it.

Many people have told us how nervous they get when they have to speak in front of others. They truly feel they turn beet red when they speak, their hearts pound so hard they can be heard, what they say does not make sense, and so on and so forth. We hear this all the time. We often record people on DVDs and play the recordings back for them to see. Most are stunned at what they see and hear. No red faces, no hearts coming out of their chests and messages that make sense. The camera does not lie.

There is something else we want to say about the folded-arms experiment. When we ask others to try it, we often hear some people immediately say they cannot do it. They do it because the reality is they can. They mistakenly think they cannot do something because the feeling of discomfort is so strong.

Are there significant opportunities you are not taking advantage of because you feel uncomfortable and feel you cannot do something? We have suggestions that can help decrease the disparity you may feel at times in the sections under **Feedback** and **Step Outside Your Comfort Zone**. In the meantime, promise us you will not let disparity create disasters in your mind.

DISASTERS

We are surprised at the attention people give to situations that have yet to happen. We hear, "What if I forget what I want to say?" "What if the equipment breaks down?" "What if I run out of time before I say what I need to say?" The way they say these statements makes it sound as though these are things that could have disastrous consequences.

There is a Chinese proverb that says the beginning of wisdom is to call things by their right names. Start thinking of these situations as possibilities rather than disasters. You can prepare for anything that is within the realm of possibilities. Equipment does break down, people forget at times, and time runs out.

You have probably seen all of those situations happen to others. You may have even thought how glad you were the situations were not happening to you. You probably paid much more attention to how the person handled the situation than the situation itself.

- Equipment does break down. Always try it out before you use it no matter how many times you have used it before. Do this before you present or before the meeting begins. If you are presenting somewhere other than your workplace, find out whom you need to call if you have technical difficulties. Have a Plan B for the times the equipment does break down.

- People forget. Who has not forgotten what they are going to say at times? When you read the information under **Pause**, you will learn about the best advice to help you when that happens. If that does not work, you will learn under **Notes** it is fine to take a look at them.

- Time runs out. You may have twenty minutes to present information at a meeting. You have two minutes left and you are only half-way through. What do you do when this happens? We know what lots of people do. They speed up and often address this reality by saying, "If I had more time …" They knew how much time they had. The information under **Time** will be of great use to you for this real possibility.

- An earthquake occurs during your presentation. That is a disaster.

You can handle any disaster—no, we mean possibilities—when you have a plan in place for how to prevent or correct the more common ones. Your confidence increases when you handle these situations without skipping a beat.

Yes You Can!

DISPARITY

- When you feel you are outside of your comfort zone, avoid letting comfort be your guide. Most of the time when you are feeling uncomfortable, you may be communicating in a way that is new and probably more effective.

- Ask for feedback from friends, family and co-workers when you are feeling uncomfortable. Are they seeing what you are feeling or has Disparity taken over?

DISASTERS

- Think back on disasters in communication situations that have happened to you that you handled well. What did you do?

_____

_____

_____

_____

_____

- When you suspect the worst-case scenario may occur, get prepared beforehand. Make a list of steps you can take if this possibility occurs. At least you will not be caught off guard and you will already have an action plan in place.

POSSIBILITIES	MY SOLUTIONS

Add any other ideas you have for yourself

_____

_____

_____

_____

_____

_____

ENDINGS

We told you how you begin a meeting, face-to-face conversation or a presentation can have an impact on the outcome. The same can be said for how you end that meeting, conversation or presentation.

MEETINGS

Do you ever feel you meet just to figure out why you are meeting? If you do not have specific action steps at the end of a meeting, you most likely will be meeting again and again to rehash the same topics. The ending of a meeting should always include:

- A recap of key decisions
- An agreement on action steps and the responsible parties
- A preview of next steps

FACE-TO-FACE CONVERSATIONS

When you are asking someone to take action, this conversation should be treated the same as a meeting. Just as we stated with meetings, the conversation should end with:

- A recap of key decisions
- An agreement on action steps and the responsible parties
- A preview of next steps

PRESENTATIONS

The last words you say should be what you want your audience to remember. Avoid doing anything that causes them to check out before you end. Avoid saying "in conclusion." That statement tells your audience they can begin to mentally shut down.

Imagine if Abraham Lincoln had said "in conclusion" before he got to the last sentence of the Gettysburg Address, where he envisions "a government of the people, by the people, for the people …" People may have been looking at their pocket watches and gathering their papers rather than catching the power of those words.

How can you end a presentation to influence your audience to take action? Your ending is your opportunity to deliver a clear, concise recap of what you want them to do. Here are some examples of effective recaps.

- "Remember practice makes permanent. By the end of today, decide which three skills you are going to practice and how you can begin each of them by the end of the week."

- "Meetings can be efficiently managed. Distribute an agenda three days prior to your next meeting and refer to it throughout."

Compare those examples to the generic, wishy-washy endings we often hear that sound similar to this: "Thank you for being here. I hope what I have shared with you has been helpful. If you have any other questions, give me a call or send me an email."

The words you use will have an impact on your success.

EYES !

People consistently tell us they are comfortable with eye contact and are good at it. Many times when they tell us this, they are not even looking at us. When we see them talking to a group, we see they are generally scanning faces rather than having any real contact.

Most people do not know how to make eye contact in a way that engages others. The main reason is they have been given bad advice about what to do with their eyes when presenting to groups of people. They have been told to:

- Look over the top of peoples' heads
- Pick a spot in the back of the room and look at it
- Find the friendly faces and stick with them
- Quickly scan faces

Have you ever received such advice? If so, it was probably given with good intent. The person who gave it to you hoped it would make you less nervous. In reality it can make you more nervous if there is not a connection between you and your audience.

If you are looking over heads or at a spot on the wall in the back of the room, you will never have a sense of whether your message is being heard. This is because you will be talking into thin air or talking to a wall. If you only look at the friendly faces, you run a high risk of leaving out those who are the decision-makers or the influencers. Plus, these individuals may grow weary of being singled out. You will look like an oscillating fan to your audience if you quickly scan faces instead of making a true connection. When you scan rather than connect, all you will see is a sea of indistinguishable faces.

Most people are more comfortable having one-to-one conversations than speaking to a group. You can have one-to-one conversations with a group of people. You can do that by looking at a person, completing a sentence with that person and then switching your eyes to someone else.

Imagine you are at a meeting with three other people and you are telling them how to use effective eye contact. You would say the first sentence of the previous paragraph to one person, the second sentence to the second person and the third sentence to the third person. This completion of a sentence is enough time to connect with a person but not so much time as to make the person or you uncomfortable.

There are significant benefits to connecting with your audience with your eyes. A major one is trust. Parents often ask children to look them in the eye to gauge whether they are telling them the truth. If you cannot look your audience in the eye, they may question whether they can trust you.

Eye contact with your audience can help you remember what you want to say. We often see people looking up at the ceiling when they lose their train of thought. There is nothing there that will ever help. The longer you lose eye contact with your audience the longer it will take you to get back on track. We know people who have had improvisational training. One of the techniques they are told to do if they do not know what to say is to look at their audience.

Effective eye contact will keep both you and your audience engaged. We once had an individual tell us he was suffering from jet lag. His employer had enrolled him in our workshop. He assumed it would be like other workshops he had attended—a good opportunity for a two-day nap. Instead, he told us, he had been engaged the entire time because we looked at people when we talked.

What about when you are having a conversation with just one person? Here is the key to effective eye contact no matter whether you are talking to one person or twenty: Only speak when you see eyes. All other times pause. We will give you tips under the **Pause** section on why we recommend this and how to do it.

It is imperative you use your eyes to:

- Create trust
- Stay on track with your message
- Engage your audience

Isn't this what your audience should expect from you if you are asking them to take action? What else might they expect?

EXPECTATIONS

Remember there is only one person that expects you to be perfect anytime you are in the room with one or more individuals. That person is you.

Under **Audience**, we indicated one of the questions you should ask yourself is what your audience's expectations are. We can guess what one of their expectations will be. They will expect you to be prepared. Not perfect. Not having all the answers. Prepared.

Being prepared is critical to feeling confident. When you have a realistic understanding of what is expected of you, you can be at your best. If you set your own expectations too high rather than at a realistic level, you risk fear creeping in.

Yes You Can!

ENDINGS

- Tie your ending to your beginning when you can during your next meeting, face-to-face conversation or presentation.

  o If you begin with a story or a quote you could have a brief reference to it at the end. If you began a meeting with the Norman Vincent Peale quote, "Change your thoughts and you change your world," you could end the meeting by saying "What is your new thought today?"

EYES !

- Here are several ways to begin practicing eye contact so it becomes your new habit.

  o When you are in a different room at home than a family member, avoid carrying on a conversation from these different rooms. Go into the room where they are and talk to them.

  o Avoid talking to a menu when you are giving your order to the wait staff at a restaurant. Look at them when you are talking.

  o When you are sitting at your desk at work and someone comes into your office to have a conversation with you, speak only when you see their eyes. Avoid talking when you are looking at your computer or materials on top of your desk.

EXPECTATIONS

- Start approaching each interaction you have as an opportunity to learn something about yourself rather than one when you need to prove something to others. Your expectations will automatically change.

Add any other ideas you have for yourself

_____

_____

_____

_____

_____

_____

Fear

The comedian Jerry Seinfeld once said most people would rather be in a casket at a funeral than delivering the eulogy. His obvious point was public speaking is the number one fear of many people.

We cannot say this enough. Fear can get in the way of you being at your best. You may have heard this before. Fear stands for false evidence appearing real.

Think about what you may have already read in this book. These are a few of the areas fear can impact.

- **Attitude.** Remember the first word in the acronym is false. How will your audience see you if your attitude is based on something that is false?

- **Body Language.** The fight-or-flight response is a person's primitive, automatic reaction that prepares someone to fight or flee from a perceived threat. Imagine what your body language might look like if you were truly afraid.

  You might look like Mohammed Ali ready to throw the first punch or like an Olympic sprinter ready to take that first step to run out of the room if you let fear take over.

- **Disasters.** You probably have a whole list you have created if you are afraid.

- **Eyes**. We have had people tell us they have sat down after speaking to a group and had no idea who was sitting in the audience. This happens because they were truly afraid to look at their audience.

Influencing others to take action is the entire premise of this book. If you give in to false evidence appearing real, forget about your ability to do that.

What are some ways to conquer this false evidence?

- **Attitude**. Start thinking in terms of what you are really feeling. Rather than fear, it is more than likely nervousness. That is something you can do something about. The techniques under **Nervousness** tell you how.

- If you have already read **Body Language, Disasters** and **Eyes**, you are aware of techniques that will enable you to feel confident rather than afraid.

We have worked with thousands of individuals over the years. Many have shared with us their fear of speaking in front of groups. We have not lost one person yet. What we see is the facial expressions people have when they come to the reality, as Franklin Delano Roosevelt said, *"the only thing to fear is fear itself."* Those facial expressions are always smiles. Treating fear as it should be treated (as false evidence) is critical to being at your best.

FACIAL EXPRESSIONS

During one of our workshops, a doctor gave a presentation on the joys of family life. He never cracked a smile. He looked as though he was having an appendicitis attack. When he saw the video playback he laughed and said, "I hope my family never sees this because they will question my love for them." In our earlier conversations with him, when he would talk about his family, he would smile, laugh and his eyes would light up. We asked him why we did not see these same facial expressions when he was presenting in front of the group. He said, "The only thing I was thinking about was I want to get this over with." He let fear take over.

We talked earlier about how important it is to connect with your audience through your eyes. Facial expressions are also critical for connecting with your audience. It is easier for your audience to believe in your message if your facial expressions communicate you believe in your message. In our conversation with the doctor about his facial expressions he laughed and said, "I wonder if the group is now concerned I will be leaving my family based on what they saw."

What could he have done? First thing was to change his attitude. He should have thought of the audience and how good they would feel when he told his heartfelt story about his family. A smile has to naturally come with that thought.

Often we hear people say, "I cannot hide how I am feeling because my facial expressions give me away." Your facial expressions need to be true to your message. We are not suggesting you need to consistently smile from ear to ear. Facial expressions can show a wide range of feelings. These include happiness, excitement, concern and so on. They can also show frustration if it is legitimate. They need to be consistent with your message.

We had the pleasure of once working with a middle-aged blind woman. She was blind from birth. She told us a technique she used for ensuring peoples' facial expressions were consistent with the message they were delivering. If she heard someone say they were in agreement with something and the voice did not sound so agreeable, she would say to the person, "If I could see your face, what would your facial expression tell me." She said people would often tell her they did have some reservations about what they had just agreed to. Even without having the ability to see someone, she understood the impact someone's facial expression would have on an audience's belief in a message.

This woman was giving her colleagues feedback on how they communicated. Feedback is critical in helping you communicate at your best.

FEEDBACK !

As we have previously mentioned, we always ask people how they would like to be perceived by others when they communicate. Their answers give us the information we need to give balanced feedback to each person. Balanced feedback means giving positive comments (keep doing what you are doing) and constructive suggestions (consider making this change).

We are not patting ourselves on the back when we tell you people love our feedback. They often tell us it is the first time they have received honest feedback on how others perceive them. They also tell us we tell it like it is in a manner that is supportive of them.

When we end our time with our audience, we always ask the person or group to create an action plan of the items they will work on, when and how they will do that, and how they will continue to receive feedback. From our experience, seeking balanced feedback is the key to your success in being at your best.

How can you seek balanced feedback? Assume someone approaches you after a meeting or presentation and says, "Nice job. You did well." You thank the person and that is the end of the conversation. What have you been told that can help you? Your guess is as good as ours. Was this feedback a result of your clear message? Or did it mean you had a great smile and put the audience at ease? Did it mean that everyone knows how to take the action you requested? Or did it mean the lunch you provided was top notch?

We are not suggesting you stop that person from leaving until you get the specifics. You do not need to grill the person—"Exactly what do you mean by that?" What we are suggesting is you actively seek out meaningful, balanced feedback.

You can do this for any face-to-face situation. Prior to a meeting or presentation, ask someone who is attending to give you feedback on a specific item. Ask the person to comment on your use of eye contact. Or ask for feedback on the beginning and ending statements you make. Here is the key: Do not just ask "Tell me how I did?" Be specific on what you want. And only ask for feedback on one item. Why? Because if you ask for feedback on eye contact, beginning and ending statements, facial expressions, the benefits you provide as incentive to the audience and how you use visual aids, you risk not hearing it all.

Here is the best way to solicit feedback to help you be at your best.

- As we stated, ask for specific feedback on one item from someone. Ask the person to describe exactly what you said or did.

- Ensure the person knows what you are asking. For instance, if you ask someone to give you feedback on your eye contact, explain exactly what your eye contact should look like.

- Be open to the feedback. For example, you may be told you occasionally looked at the ceiling while you talked. Rather than saying you did not do it as often as you have in the past, thank the person for the feedback.

- After you receive the feedback, consider:

    o How the feedback differed from how you perceived you did

o What you will continue to do as a result

o What you will change as a result

o What you learned about yourself while receiving the feedback

o What your comfort level was in receiving this feedback

What if you do not agree with the feedback you receive? You still thank the person for giving it to you. You make the decision whether or not to make a change. We always ask for feedback from our audiences and we always take it to heart. That does not mean we always change our behavior based on the comments. Feedback is a description of someone else's perception of your behavior and the effect the behavior had on that person. There are times we change how we present based on feedback we receive and there are times we do not. We make that decision on whether the feedback helps us be at our best.

There is another benefit of receiving feedback. It can help strengthen relationships. It adds to your ability to influence others to take action if your audience sees you value their perceptions of you.

Yes You Can!

FEAR

- Ask yourself: "If fear wasn't a factor, what change would you make in your life?"

- Did you take this question seriously? If not, why not?

FACIAL EXPRESSIONS

- Have you ever received feedback on what your facial expressions communicate? If not, what is stopping you from asking for feedback?

- If possible, record yourself to see if your facial expressions are consistent with your message during a presentation or during a practice session for an upcoming face-to-face conversation.

FEEDBACK !

- After you receive constructive feedback from others, use the form on the following page to begin taking action for your development.

Feedback you receive	Items you will work on	When and how you will do this?	How will you continue to receive feedback?

Add any other ideas you have for yourself

_____

_____

_____

_____

_____

_____

GESTURES

There is a very funny film called *Talladega Nights* that stars Will Ferrell. He plays a race car driver named Ricky Bobby. At one point in the film Ricky Bobby is being interviewed by a TV reporter. His hands are flailing all over the place and he says something like, "I don't know what the heck to do with these hands."

We have heard so many people tell us that very same thing. Others tell us they have been told they use their hands too much. In either case, the result is often the same. They go to extremes by trying to find ways to not use their hands. They cross their arms, clasp their hands, put their hands in their pockets, put their arms behind their backs, carry a pen (or a cup) as a crutch, play with their jewelry or hair or ball their hands into fists. All of this is done to give themselves something to do with their hands or to prevent themselves from using their hands too much. Do not go to those extremes. What should you do? Gesture appropriately.

How should you gesture? Everyone will gesture differently. There is not a formula that says you should have one gesture every three sentences. The key is to put yourself in a position that your gestures are appropriate to your message. Here are tips to let that happen for you.

- Adopt a neutral resting position. By resting position, we mean where to place your arms and hands when you are not gesturing. If you are standing, your arms should be relaxed at your sides with your hands open. If seated, your hands should be relaxed and open.

- When you gesture, make the action deliberate. If you are using a gesture to illustrate how high expenses are, let your gesture stay in that position for a moment so your audience can take it in. When you are finished making your point, go back to that neutral resting position.

- Use a variety of gestures. Use one hand or both at times. The key is gestures must be appropriate to the words.

- Keep objects out of your hands unless there is a reason for them. We have seen people hold full cups of coffee in their hands while gesturing. All we were thinking about was when the coffee was going to fly out of the cup. We have seen someone play with a paper clip the entire time he was talking. All we were paying attention to was the sculpture he was creating. If you are using markers, put them down when you are finished. If you have a remote for your laptop and need to use it often, place it in the palm of your hand in a way that you can still gesture.

- Avoid pointing at people with your index finger. Use an open palm instead.

Why should you gesture? Gestures can help:

- Add emphasis to your message
- Grab your audience's attention
- Create a picture for your audience
- Make your points memorable
- Help you relax

When people are relaxed, they gesture. You can see it when friends are telling stories to one another. You can see it when people are talking on the phone. Under **Facial Expressions** we spoke of the blind woman we worked with. When she introduced herself in front of the other participants, she used appropriate gestures for things she had never seen. In fact, she was the only person in that group who did not try to find ways to limit or eliminate her gestures. She had never seen the bad habits people adopt.

This book is all about influencing others to take action. Appropriate gestures can help you do that. Because of the visual image they create, they make it much easier for people to get the point you are making. How else can you get to the point?

GET TO THE POINT

Considering what this section is called, we thought about simply saying get to the point and nothing more. We realized it is not that simple for people to do. We base that on what we hear on a daily basis. We often ask people at the end of our workshops, what one skill are they going to work on for the next three weeks. More than once, we have heard people say something along these lines: "I am going to work on not saying more than I need to say. A lot of times I give details that are not needed and I tend to make the same point over and over and even then people do not always get what I am asking them to do. I want to eliminate all of the unnecessary filler stuff." We will nod and say, "What is it that you are going to work on?" They always get the point we are making and will answer with a smile, *"I am going to be concise."*

If you are trying to influence others to take action, it will be easier if you eliminate the irrelevant information. The more you say that is unnecessary, the greater the risk people will either miss or misinterpret the point.

What can help you get to the point?

- Stay focused. When you find yourself going down the path of saying too much and you begin to feel like a train about to derail, put the brakes on and get yourself back on track. See the section under **Pause** on how to do this.

- **Keep your objective in mind.** Think in terms of what your audience needs to know about what you want them to do, not what you want to tell them. Have the confidence to realize you do not need to tell them everything you know in order to influence them.

- **Put thought to your words.** We once had a scientist in a program who told us he had a very hard time explaining what he did in a way people could understand. We asked him to give it a try. He immediately started talking for about two minutes using words that were meaningless to us. We asked him to try again but in half the time and without the jargon. He started talking right away and we were still lost. Then we asked him to tell us in fifteen words or less. He did something different that time. He thought about it for a few seconds and told us: "I research drugs to be approved that provide health benefits for children." He had a big smile on his face because he could see we got it and he did too. He realized he had to think about it before he said something. What a unique concept, huh? Thinking before you talk.

- **Use the concept of the Rule of Three.** Focus your message on no more than the three most significant points. It is easier for people to get the point and it is easier for them to remember it. We have asked groups to name the original Three Stooges (Larry, Moe and Shemp, according to Wikipedia). After someone is able to name them, we ask that same person to name the Seven Dwarves. We have had individuals say, "That's not as easy to remember." Precisely.

- **Pay attention to your audience.** Are they hanging on your every word or are they dazed? Are they attentive or are they fidgeting? It is fine if you get the occasional question asking you to repeat or clarify something. If those are the only types of questions you get, that could be telling you something.

To summarize all we have said, get to the point.

Yes You Can!

GESTURES

- Read **Gestures** again. It is all there for you.

GET TO THE POINT

In addition to the ideas under **Get to the Point**, try the following.

- Tell a favorite story. Now tell it in half the time. Ask yourself was it really necessary to say everything the first time.

- Cut your meeting time by saying less about each agenda item.

- Reserve your meeting room for a maximum of 50 minutes.

Add any other ideas you have for yourself

_____

_____

_____

_____

_____

_____

Habits

"Habit is habit and not to be flung out of the window by any man, but coaxed downstairs a step at a time."

– Mark Twain

Throughout this book we are showing you how you can be at your very best. Breaking your old communication habits is one of the critical steps to make this happen.

It is important not to commit to changing everything at once. As Mark Twain said, start with smaller steps. Changing habits takes time and you have to be in the right mind set; determined to go the extra mile. It takes seventeen to twenty-one days to change a habit, depending on whom you talk to or what you read.

Habits are never easy to break. At first you will feel uncomfortable, maybe even unsure of the decision you have made to change a habit. This is where the true test of your determination and willpower will occur. When you are communicating a message and trying to incorporate your new communication behaviors, will you roll up your sleeves and diligently push forward with your new behaviors or will you go back to your more comfortable old habits?

You will need to work on your new habits to the point where they become something you do not have to think about. Then and only then will you be at your very best. Think of a hobby or activity you enjoy doing. If it is golf, you know when your stroke is right on. If it is tennis, you know it when you hit the sweet spot. If it is honoring your commitment to take fifteen minutes a day to truly relax by listening to your favorite music, you know it when you think there is no better sound than what you are listening to. There is the feeling of "this is it!"

What about your communication habits do you want to change first to be at your very best? Always have this goal in mind: Take action today. Use the list under the **Yes You Can!** section for **Habits** to put in priority order what you would like to work on. Once you have identified your priorities, make a commitment. Make changes in all of your face-to-face conversations, not just those you have at work. To break a habit means you have to be consistent.

At the end of the day it comes down to the choices you make. Do not be afraid to make the right one.

HUMOR

We invited an attorney to a workshop when we needed someone to speak on the legal ramifications of a subject. The audience included attorneys, human resource managers and state legislators. We educated him on the demographics, knowledge level and needs of the audience. To our dismay, he began his presentation with a joke mocking attorneys. Our dismay increased as he continued to tell several more. You could feel the dynamics in the room immediately change. At the first break, more than half of the audience left.

When used well, humor can add energy to a room. When used inappropriately, it can cast a pall over the room.

Appropriate humor is a great way to create a relationship with your audience. Use natural humor. By that we mean, make fun of yourself, play off what the audience says, and have fun with the audience.

There are many benefits to using appropriate humor.

- You can grab and keep an audience's attention.

- It can help you relax. This in turn helps your audience relax.

- It can help increase your audience's retention of important points.

- Humor helps animate you through facial expressions and gestures.

- When used appropriately, it can give both you and your audience a break from complex or difficult subjects.

What should you avoid?

- Telling jokes. We both cringe when we hear someone say "I would like to start with a joke." In most cases, the person is not a good joke teller, the joke is not funny, the joke has nothing to do with the subject, or in the worst-case scenario (as with our attorney friend) it is offensive.

- Letting humor completely obscure your points.

You can add humor to many topics. This does not mean you are not taking your subject seriously. What it does mean is that you can have some fun with it. We speak with authority here. One of us used to teach tax law and one of us used to teach accounting principles. Our best advice to you is start having fun with what you are learning from this book.

Yes You Can!

HABITS

HABITS YOU WANT TO CHANGE	WHEN WILL YOU MAKE THIS CHANGE?	HOW WILL YOU GET FEEDBACK?

HUMOR

- Select a subject you think is dry or boring and add humor to it.

- Think about what made you laugh recently. How can you add this to your subject?

Add any other ideas you have for yourself

_____

_____

_____

_____

_____

_____

INTRODUCTIONS

We stated under **Beginnings** that they are your opportunities to make a connection with your audience.

We suggested you use the concepts of connecting, asking for interaction and telling your audience what is in it for them. It did not include your introduction. We are going to say something that may seem contrary to what you and most others have done in the past. Introducing yourself is not the first thing you need to do. There are a number of reasons why we say this.

- Someone has already introduced you.

- Your biography is printed on the agenda.

- You have introduced yourself while greeting individuals when they arrived.

When should you introduce yourself? Right after your beginning statement, share your background, and when you do keep the following in mind.

- Adapt your background to the experience level, industry, knowledge or needs of your audience. If you have similar experiences in a particular industry, share that. For the times you do not have the experience, ask yourself what do you have to offer. The answer is you have the knowledge level to meet their needs.

- Keep it brief.

What you say during your introduction is one way to grab attention and build credibility. How you sound will also create credibility, which takes us to inflection.

INFLECTION

How you feel about your message will be heard through your vocal inflection. Are you excited, passionate, concerned or serious? We have found most people struggle with how they use their voice, and as a result they often communicate the wrong message.

To avoid this type of misinterpretation, be aware of the words you emphasize. Read the following sentence out loud six times, emphasizing a different word each time. "I did not eat the cake." What did you notice? Changing the emphasis from one word to another will change the meaning of your sentence. Therefore, you need to make sure you are emphasizing words that convey the meaning you intend. You want people to understand what you are saying. It is more than words; it is how they are conveyed.

On numerous occasions people will tell us they feel they speak in a monotone. They may have received feedback from their audience that they sounded bored or lethargic at times.

One of our clients asked us to observe his communication during a staff meeting. The purpose of the meeting was to congratulate over 100 employees on a successful year and to motivate them for the upcoming year. As we observed him present his message to his team, he stated the following in a boring, monotonous voice with no facial expressions, "Congratulations on a job well done. Some of you will receive bonuses. Others will receive pay increases. Keep up the good work." During his lame speech we watched the energy deflate throughout the room. We saw confused facial expressions and employees nudging each other as if they were saying, "is he serious?" Our client created confusion rather than motivation.

Several things can cause your voice to lack inflection. Many people do not know how to correct this without sounding phony, although most could do it naturally with a little conscious effort. These are some of the things we saw with our client. He had his arms crossed the entire time and he did not pause between sentences. The periods we added above to what he said did not exist when he spoke. He began every sentence with the word "uh" or "and".

Gestures and facial expressions would have given his voice more inflection. Use them when you deliver any message.

We are not suggesting you should sound as if you are speaking on an infomercial. We are recommending you use your inflection to add credibility to your message. Place emphasis on the words you want your audience to hear and remember.

Your voice is a powerful instrument. Make it work for you, not against you.

INTEGRITY !

Webster's dictionary defines integrity as the state of honesty and sincerity. Most people we have asked define integrity along those lines. We believe those traits are important and we cover that under **Authenticity**. You may be surprised to find this is not the primary definition in our copy of Webster's dictionary. The primary definition of integrity is that it is the quality or state of being complete.

In order to be at your best, you have to be complete in every aspect that plays a part in your communication. That means having integrity. That is why we have used **!** to highlight what we feel is needed to have you be complete when you want to influence others. We have taken great care in deciding which areas to highlight. When we look back at our own successes when we were at our best, every one of those areas played a part. When we are only good at something, we guarantee you it is because we have let one of these areas slide.

Tiger Woods is not always at his best. Neither are most of us. You can increase the percentage in your relationships by having integrity.

Yes You Can!

INTRODUCTION

- Practice adapting your background to different audiences. Compare how you would you tell CEOs, a first grade class or new employees at your company what you do.

INFLECTION

- Add bigger gestures to increase your inflection.

- Read a children's book out loud and add emphasis throughout the story.

- Audiotape yourself while you are talking on the phone at work or at home.

- Ask for feedback from friends, family members and peers to tell you when your voice sounds monotonous or needs more enthusiasm.

INTEGRITY !

- Review this book when you have finished reading it. Are the items marked with ! always a part of your communication? If there are ones you feel are often lacking, add them to the habits you want to change.

Add any other ideas you have for yourself

_____

_____

_____

_____

_____

_____

Journey

"Continual improvement is an unending journey."

— Lloyd Dobyns and Clare Crawford-Mason,
Thinking About Quality

We have had the opportunity to work with highly skilled individuals. They may be the types of individuals who, when you think of the best communicators, you know they would be those people. Other people may wonder why these individuals need to work with us. We know why. They come to us asking us to make them better because they know being at their best means never standing still. They are constantly on a journey to keep up with change, to improve their skills and to have another opportunity to practice influencing others to take action.

These highly skilled individuals understand being at their best does not mean being satisfied with the status quo. We are constantly blown away because we see these individuals at their best and yet when they leave they always say, "I will be back for more." They understand there is always something to learn. They are always searching and discovering.

Personal change happens through a journey of discovery. You need to find out more about yourself: how you communicate, how you interact with others and how you may have been limiting yourself. Along the way you will find out a lot more about how you can be in charge.

Be willing to take your own journey. Use this book to help you:

- Get prepared for your journey
- See things in a new way
- Discover the positive resources you already have available
- Learn lessons and new skills along the way

Your journey started when you were a kid. We guarantee some of what you learned then can still help you be at your best.

Yes You Can!

JOURNEY

- List some of the major milestones in your life. What did you learn that can assist you to be at your best?

MILESTONE	WHAT IS MOST MEMORABLE?	HOW CAN I USE THAT AS I CONTINUE MY JOURNEY?

Add any other ideas you have for yourself

_____

_____

_____

_____

_____

_____

KIDS

"Children have imagination, a quality that seems to flicker out in so many adults."

– Jacqueline Kennedy

In addition to imagination, we have seen other things seem to flicker out in adults. Those things include curiosity, creativity and the ability to step outside of one's comfort zone.

We have yet to ask for volunteers in our workshops and had to choose from a multitude of hands shooting up in the air asking to be first. You know if you ask for volunteers in a kindergarten class, almost all hands shoot up and they usually have no clue what they are being asked to do. What happened to make most adults fear to do something even in front of a supportive audience?

We do an exercise involving diaphragmatic breathing. We find less than a third of our participants breathe properly. Watch babies while they are on their backs, breathing perfectly from their bellies rather than from their upper chests. It is a much healthier method of breathing and is the type of breathing that can help lessen anxiety. When did this ability disappear for most adults?

How many of you have been talking to a child when the child cups your face with his or her hands and turns your face so you are truly looking at the child. Children get the fact we need to look at someone when we talk. When did we stop doing that?

Watch children when they first start walking. They do not put their hands in their pockets or behind their backs. They stand tall, or at least as tall as they can. When did we start slouching or wringing our hands when we stand?

When you were a child, how many times did you ask "why" to just about anything anyone said? Okay, we agree there has to be some balance. Have there been times when someone has resisted something you have asked them to do? Rather than asking why you may have made a false assumption about the reason. Curiosity at times can give you information that can help you ultimately be successful in influencing someone.

There are many life lessons we can learn from others, including children. We know it is not children who made Robert Fulghum's book, *All I Really Need to Know I Learned in Kindergarten,* a best seller for many years. If any of you have read Dr. Seuss or Shel Silverstein's books to your children, you know you can learn lessons from them also.

We had a gentleman in a program who told us he carried a picture of himself as a 6-year-old. It was a picture of him looking with great curiosity and excitement at something in his hand. The man said he has no idea what the object was. He carried the picture because he wanted to remind himself that learning something new can be exciting.

Think back on your childhood and think of traits you could use to be at your best: a sense of imagination, curiosity, creativity, not being afraid to step outside of your comfort zone and standing tall.

We are not asking you to act childish. We are asking you to rediscover that sense of imagination, curiosity or joy. These are qualities that can help you influence others to take action. A good part of rediscovery is new knowledge.

KNOWLEDGE !

We once listened to a speaker deliver a keynote presentation and immediately knew we had heard it before. We had seen him five years previously. To our surprise he was still delivering the same message. For five years he did not bother to learn anything new that would have made his presentation more meaningful. He lost all credibility with us.

We have heard people say professionals are always in school. They are always looking to learn. Knowledge is power because it adds to your credibility and provides continuous education for yourself. It is not about knowing everything there is to know. It is about keeping current and up-to-date. Believe it or not, this does not take a lot of time. Here is how to make this happen.

- Know your audience.

    o   If you need to, refer back to the section under **Audience.**

- Know your subject.

    o   The reality is, if you are not prepared with your subject, everything in this book is useless.

    o   Tie your knowledge of your subject to current events, which gives you instant credibility.

- Know current events.

    o   Read newspaper headlines.

    o   Read Internet home pages such as Yahoo or MSN.

o If you see something that may relate to your audience, read that newspaper story or Internet site and share the highlights.

o Read company websites, newsletters or blogs.

It is always important your audience knows you have taken the time to learn what you need to know before you ask them to take action. Doing the things we have suggested will greatly reduce the risk of any audience questioning your credibility as we did with the keynote presenter.

We offer a cautionary note about knowledge. Always remember others have knowledge also. Malcolm Forbes once said, "*The dumbest people I know are those who know it all.*" One way to find out what others know is to listen.

Yes You Can!

KIDS

- Observe the behavior of children. What makes them likable, creative and curious?

- How can you apply these behaviors?

KNOWLEDGE !

- Learn at least one new thing a day and decide how you can use it.

- Schedule time during the day for learning. Even if it is only fifteen minutes.

Add any other ideas you have for yourself

_____

_____

_____

_____

_____

_____

73

LISTENING !

Being an effective listener is crucial to your ability to influence others to take action. Whether you are giving a presentation, conducting a meeting or having a face-to-face conversation, chances are, you are missing opportunities to influence action. Being a good listener means you have curiosity about what someone says.

To test your own listening efficiency, think about how often you ask someone to repeat information, or how many times someone has said to you, "You're not listening to me." This happens more than you might think because most people only listen for the first three to four seconds of a conversation.

Being a good listener means you are not:

- Thinking about what you are going to say next
- Making assumptions of what someone will say
- Disagreeing with what you are hearing before someone finishes
- Allowing yourself to be distracted by work
- Thinking about what happened earlier in the day
- Allowing personal feelings to get in the way
- Interrupting people before they are finished talking

The way you can avoid doing any of these common habits is to have a sense of curiosity. How do you add curiosity to your listening skills?

- Make solid eye contact. We state under **Questions** this shows your audience you are listening to them and helps you stay focused on what is being communicated.

- Pause before answering. A pause often encourages others to provide you with additional information.

- Listen for changes in tone of voice, inflection or projection.

- Be patient when listening to what is said and avoid interrupting, even though you may believe what someone is saying is wrong or irrelevant. Indicate simple acceptance, not necessarily agreement, by nodding or perhaps injecting an occasional "I see."

- Encourage others to provide additional information with a phrase such as, "Tell me more."

- Take notes to capture key points and ideas.

We are making the assumption you can probably identify only a few people in your life you feel are good listeners. We guarantee these individuals live and breathe these skills every day. They are truly connected to their audiences. You should always strive to make that connection. Something that can be a barrier to connecting is how people often use a lectern.

LECTERN

There may be times when you present information to a large group and you have the option of using a lectern. Only use it if truly necessary. We can think of two times.

- You are the President of the United States and are delivering the State of the Union address.

- You are valedictorian of your college and are delivering your speech.

There may be other times, but more often than not, people use a lectern as a crutch. You can usually tell the signs. They lean on it. They constantly read their notes and rarely look at their audience. They clutch the sides of the lectern.

Take control of the room set-up. Ask the conference coordinator for a wireless lavaliere microphone so you do not have to be stuck behind a lectern.

If you find yourself in a situation when you absolutely have to use a lectern, use these tips.

- Step an inch back from it and stand up straight.

- Rest your hands on the shelf rather than clutching the sides. This allows for natural gestures.

- Use big gestures that can be seen by all.

- Place your notes on the shelf of the lectern. When you need to refer to them, pause with confidence. Only speak when you are looking at your audience.

Most importantly, do not let the lectern become a crutch. Step out from behind it when at all possible and use purposeful movement.

Yes You Can!

LISTENING !

- At the end of the day write down at least one new idea you have heard someone else say. If you are not able to do this, this could be a sign you may not be an effective listener.

- Immediately following a face-to-face conversation, ask yourself what you remember.

LECTERN

- If you use a lectern, step away from it the next time you deliver a presentation.

- Watch for other physical barriers you may be hiding behind. Avoid sitting behind your desk during a face-to-face conversation. Instead pull up a chair and sit next to the person on occasion.

Add any other ideas you have for yourself

_____

_____

_____

_____

_____

_____

Movement

"Thoughts come clearly while one walks."

— Thomas Mann

We are surprised at how many people we see get up in front of a group to speak and do one of two things. They will stand perfectly still as though their feet are stuck in cement or they move without purpose. Movement without purpose includes pacing, rocking back and forth or stepping backwards from the audience. It seems they have lost their ability to walk and talk at the same time.

We recommend purposeful movement when you are presenting to a group. It will:

- Channel your nervous energy, help you relax and focus on your audience

- Keep your audience engaged and connected

There are several steps that will help you accomplish the benefits of purposeful movement.

- Look first at one person then move towards them.

- Keep your eyes locked on that person as you are moving towards them.

- When you have reached your destination, stop and plant your feet and look at someone else.

- Stand in place for at least three sentences to avoid pacing.

Moving with purpose is another skill that will help influence others to take action. Your thoughts will become clearer to your audience when you move with purpose. Doing most things with a purpose in mind is beneficial. Having a true purpose for a meeting and using it to guide the time spent at the meeting can help you get what you want.

MEETINGS

How many hours a week do you spend in meetings? We have read numerous statistics. One article stated executives average 23 hours per week in meetings. Another stated 18 and yet another stated 26. Whatever the number is, we suspect meetings are a significant portion of your life.

In spite of the fact meetings have gone on since the beginning of time, every article or book we read emphasizes that a sizable portion of the time spent is unproductive.

If a sizable amount of time is unproductive, imagine the effect on those attending the meeting. They may be tired, frustrated or agreeing to actions only in hopes the meeting will end. This is not the best scenario for influencing others to take action. We have heard managers talk about their frustration of people seemingly agreeing to something and then not carrying out the expected actions.

Bookstores and libraries have a hefty amount of shelf space devoted to books and articles about holding successful meetings. The last time we did an Internet search for meetings, we received 142,000,000 references.

We will save you time by reiterating suggestions in an A to Z listing. We feel these suggestions are the most important when you need to influence others to take action.

- Agendas are distributed at least 24 hours ahead of time.

- Begin on time.

- Consensus should be used when total group buy-in is imperative.

- Define roles (timekeeper, scribe, etc.) at the beginning.

- End on time.

- Focus on the goals of the meeting throughout to ensure its success.

- Ground rules are the way to help the process of a meeting.

- Handouts should be used for items that do not need discussion.

- Interruptions. Turn off cell phones, Blackberries, Trios, computers or anything else that causes unnecessary interruptions.

- Jokes are rarely appropriate humor at a meeting.

- Keep it short.

- Latecomers should be brought up to speed ASAP with only what is necessary.

- Monitor progress of next steps agreed to at the meeting.

- Neatness counts. Start and end with a clean room.

- One person speaks at a time.

- Post this list for others to see.

- Quiet time should be used to think before important decisions are made.

- Require all attending the meeting participate in some manner.

- Schedule meetings at mid-morning when possible; people are at their best.

- Thank people for their time and input.

- Use email, memos, and phone calls if all you need to do is provide information.

- Visualize a successful meeting.

- Who should be there? Be selective.

- eXamine how things went to help improve future meetings.

- You should guide the process.

- Zounds! Your meetings are productive. Pat yourself on the back.

Yes You Can!

MOVEMENT

- Here are ways you can make purposeful movement your new habit.

    o Practice movement while you are talking on your cell phone or wearing a telephone headset. On occasion, stand in place.

    o When you are presenting, arrive early to practice movement in the space you have.

MEETINGS

- Read **Meetings** again. It is all there for you.

Add any other ideas you have for yourself

_____

_____

_____

_____

_____

_____

Notes

On numerous occasions individuals will ask us if they can use their notes when they communicate a message. Our response is always, "It depends on what your notes look like and how you intend to use them." Notes should not be a script, because your intention is to have a conversation with your audience, not to deliver a monologue. It is much easier to influence others to take action when they feel you are talking to them and not at them.

We are not saying you need to use notes for every face-to-face conversation you have. Here is how notes should be used when you do need to have them available.

- Use bullet points with one to three words per bullet.

- Place your notes off to the side. Remember you can use purposeful movement to walk over and refer to your notes if you need to. When you are seated, place your notes on the table to your right or left rather than in front of you. This will force you to look at them with deliberation when you need to, as opposed to being automatically drawn to them.

- When you refer to your notes, pause and take all of the time you need to gather your thoughts.

Using notes does not only pertain to instances when presenting to a group. We recommend you practice using notes so you are comfortable with them in front of any audience. When you are referring to a meeting agenda or taking notes during a meeting, pause when you refer to them.

Always avoid holding your notes. If you hold them, you are likely to read your notes, fidget with them and use them as part of your gestures.

There are times we have used our notes. We have asked members of our audience what perception they had of us when they observed us using our notes. More often than not, people say, "What notes?" When you refer to your notes confidently, your audience will never think you have forgotten what to say. If they notice it at all, they will know you are referring to your notes only to ensure you deliver all of the pertinent information.

A major benefit for you when you use your notes confidently is to reduce the level of nervousness you may feel. The following gives you additional tips to control your nervousness.

NERVOUSNESS

Both of us kayak. We once watched a very experienced kayaker purposely tip his kayak over about ten times in a row. He was practicing his ability to get back into the kayak if it flipped. When we talked to him later, we told him tipping a kayak over in such a deep lake would make us nervous. He said he gets nervous every time, but only for a moment because he knows what to do about it.

Nervousness is different than fear. Remember we told you fear stands for false evidence appearing real. There is nothing false about nervousness. Like the kayaker, we certainly experience it. And just like him, we know what to do about it.

Let's start off first with what not to do. That is, to announce to the world you are nervous. We record many participants in our workshops as they practice communicating. On occasion, as people sit down from a recorded exercise, we will tell them we knew they were nervous and ask them if they know how we knew that. They usually say we must have guessed it because they were rambling or turning red or all kinds of other things they felt was a sure give-away. We always say no and ask the rest of the group how we knew it. They always know the answer. It is because people tell us. In the middle of a sentence or as they sit down, they announce how nervous they are. Rather than announce it to the world, do something about it.

You can turn nervousness into animation and energy that works for you. Here are some ways to do it.

- Immediately turn your attention to your audience.
- Use facial expressions, gestures and purposeful movement.
- Pause and breathe.

Occasionally we will have people tell us they never get nervous. Our thought is that is too bad. Our feeling about nervousness is the same as what the late comedian Paul Lynde once said: *"If I ever completely lost my nervousness I would be frightened half to death."*

Yes You Can!

NOTES

- Ask for feedback after your meeting, presentation or face-to-face conversation. Are you pausing when you refer to your notes or are you having a conversation with your notes?

- Always take the time to silently read all you need when you refer to your notes.

NERVOUSNESS

- Start telling yourself it is okay to feel nervous. Turn your nervousness into energy by applying the skills we recommend under this section.

- Stop telling your audience you are nervous.

Add any other ideas you have for yourself

_____

_____

_____

_____

_____

OBJECTIVE !

Being at your very best begins with being clear about the results you want to achieve. This involves clarifying your objective. Part of this clarification means understanding your audience, knowing what action steps you want your audience to take, and knowing the benefits of what you are asking of them. This information will then inspire you to determine how to communicate your message for maximum impact. Sounds simple, doesn't it? You may be surprised to know the majority of individuals we work with make clarifying their objective the last step when designing their message. If you do not know where you are going, how will you get there?

When we wrote this book our objective was to provide you with techniques on how to influence action. On occasion we needed to go back to our objective as we felt ourselves beginning to stray in an opposite direction. There were times we really wanted to include something we had written, but then asked ourselves how it related to our objective and realized we were missing the point.

One of our clients asked us to participate in a meeting that was being scheduled within a month. We asked her what the objective of the meeting was. Her response: "If you do not want to be there you don't need to come." We told her this was not what we were saying. We were asking what the objective was. She looked at us with confusion and responded, "I don't know. Maybe I shouldn't be calling this meeting." She ended up sending an email with information she needed others to simply be aware of. How many times have you gone to a meeting and wondered before, during and after, "What the heck was that about?"

If you do not know your objective, how can you be clear about the results you want to achieve? If you are not clear, can your audience be clear? There is a risk your audience may begin to make up stories about what you want to achieve. Stories can be a good thing, but not when they are made up.

ONCE UPON A TIME

For any of you who have ever told stories to children, you know how excited they get just by hearing the words "once upon a time." Children love good stories. So do adults.

There are many benefits to you if you tell good stories.

- You can have an immediate connection with your audience.

- Your message becomes memorable.

- You can enhance your credibility if your story is relevant not only to your point but also to the experiences of your audience.

- You can make any topic immediately interesting.

There are definite skills to telling a good story.

- It must be relevant. You do not want people scratching their heads and thinking "What is the point?"

- It must be brief. We have asked people to tell a story in half the time they originally told it. They are always able to do it. Every time it is a better story because they leave out unnecessary details.

- It must be told from your own experience. We once heard someone tell a story about his grandfather that was relevant, brief and meaningful. Two weeks later we heard someone from the same organization tell the same story. This time it was disjointed, long-winded and confusing. We later asked this person about the story. He told us it was something he had heard from the same person we heard it from. He said the story helped him understand a work policy better and he wanted to help others have the same experience.

  We suggested he could begin his story like this, "Last month I heard Jeff tell a story about his grandfather that made me think about something in a brand new way. It made my life easier. That's what I am asking you to do today. Think of something in a brand new way."

When should you use stories? In **Beginnings**, we stated they can be used to begin a presentation. They can also be used throughout the presentation, in meetings and face-to-face conversations. They just need to be relevant.

What is the best way to begin a story? You never have to say something like, "Before we begin, I would like to tell you a story." Begin with when it happened to you. For instance, "Four days ago …, Just this morning …, Two months ago, I was driving to work when …"

We have had people tell us they do not tell stories because they do not have any. Everyone has stories. You do not have to be Mark Twain. You have stories if you have had experiences, challenges, successes or failures. You have stories if you know people. What is yours?

OPPORTUNITIES !

We are so fortunate to live in a world that provides us endless opportunities. At the end of the day we decide who we want to be, what impact we want to have on others and how hard we are willing to work to get there. Take every opportunity you can to practice your new skills and communication behaviors.

To find the opportunities that will have the greatest impact on your development, you will need to seek them out. Begin by identifying what it is that is most difficult or most uncomfortable for you. Do you want to be more comfortable communicating in front of a group? Do you want to be concise and clear? Do you need to improve your ability to organize messages?

Whatever your areas of improvement are, there are a number of opportunities just waiting for you.

- Organizations at work or in your community that you can volunteer for giving you opportunities to practice your communication.

- Departmental meetings at work that give you the opportunity to lead conversations.

- Toastmasters – a non-profit educational organization that teaches public speaking and leadership skills.

- The Second City or other training centers for improvisation and acting.

Getting involved in these opportunities helps you practice your new skills and build confidence.

ORGANIZE !

Have you ever noticed the hundreds of books, articles and Internet matches there are for "how to get organized?" The topics promise *"101*

Ways to Organize Your Life," *"How to Organize Your Kitchen Cabinets"* and even *"Power Tips for Organizing Your Outlook."*

Many of us have a constant desire to get organized or to try a new, improved way. When it comes to communication, too many individuals communicate a message in their way without giving their audience an opportunity to follow along. It is no wonder miscommunication frequently occurs between speakers and their audiences. When you are not organized, you will quickly find yourself wandering in many directions and taking too much time to figure out where you are going. If you are wandering, it is easy for your audience to get lost.

The first thing you should always consider is who is the audience for whom you are designing your message. Refer back to the information under **Audience** and ask yourself the questions we presented. Next, what is your objective? When you have a crystal-clear definition of your audience and objective, you are ready to organize a message that will influence action.

To get organized and stay organized, every message needs to have a beginning, middle and ending. It is your job to communicate these components to your audience without creating confusion. You are probably familiar with the following:

- Tell them what you are going to tell them
- Tell them
- Tell them what you told them

To get your message off to a strong start that is clear and concise, refer to our suggestions under **Beginnings**. This is the "tell them what you are going to tell them" part.

Next, tell them. This will be the body of what you have to say. Communicate to your audience the key points you have identified based on their expectations. They need to know from the start how you plan to proceed. Keep your key points to three or less. You can create confusion for you and your audience if you have more. Stating your key points will provide you and your audience with a road map identifying the direction you plan on taking together.

To make your key points clear, memorable and influential, create sub-points that support your key points. It is generally a good idea to have three or fewer sub-points to support each key point.

There are several ways you can organize the middle.

- Make a chronological progression from first to last (such as steps, events, etc.) or past to present.

- List all of the pros and cons to an idea, concept or strategy.

- Propose a problem followed by a list of recommended solutions, then conclude with the best solution and explain why.

- Present a persuasive argument.

Once your key and sub-points are communicated, leave your audience with a strong and memorable ending. Tell them what you have told them. The ending needs to provide a summary of your message, a recap of your key points and the action you want your audience to take.

You rarely have a second chance to deliver your message again. You can not say to your audience, "In case you did not understand my message the first time, let's do this all over again." If you are organized, your audience will be with you the first time. No matter how organized you are, if you do not give your audience the chance to understand what you have said, you still have the possibility of losing them along the way. Pausing can prevent that from happening.

Yes You Can!

OBJECTIVE !

- Make this your #1 priority before you schedule a meeting, create your message for a presentation or participate in a face-to-face conversation.

- Ask yourself if your objective is to create awareness, to have your audience learn new skills or to implement a new process. Make sure your objective focuses only on the end result you want your audience to achieve.

ONCE UPON A TIME

- If you are not a storyteller, practice with family and friends.

- Begin with a story at your next business face-to-face conversation.

OPPORTUNITIES !

- Attend one of the organizations we suggested under **Opportunities** or find one on your own by the end of this month.

ORGANIZE !

To guarantee your message is organized in a way that makes it easy to follow from the **Beginning** to the **Ending,** use this checklist.

_____I know my **Audience** as best as I can.

_____My **Objective** is clear.

_____I grab the audience's attention in the **Beginning** of my message.

_____My **Beginning** includes relevant actions and **Benefits.**

_____My key points highlight three or fewer relevant concerns or issues.

_____My sub-points accurately support my key points and are in logical order.

_____I provide any necessary supporting facts, research and/or data.

_____My transitions make my message easy to follow and understand.

_____I will stay within the allocated time frame.

_____My **Ending** is memorable and provides a summary of my message.

Add any other ideas you have for yourself

_____

_____

_____

_____

_____

_____

PAUSE !

Imagine you are at Gettysburg, Pennsylvania in 1863 waiting to hear President Abraham Lincoln's dedication speech at the Soldiers' National Cemetery. He begins, *"Uh four score and you know seven years ago uh our fathers basically brought forth upon this continent a new nation uh actually conceived in liberty and actually dedicated to the uh proposition so that all men are created like equal but now we are engaged in a great civil war uh testing whether that nation or uh like any ..."*

We have delivered that part of his great speech just as it is written above to a number of audiences. They always laugh and come to the same conclusion. This speech would not have the impact it has if he had delivered it that way.

Read it out loud just as it is written. You should notice something. It is difficult to breathe, it is difficult to give words the emphasis they deserve, and for many, you may feel you are speaking faster than you normally do. If Abraham Lincoln had delivered the Gettysburg Address in this way, he would have felt the same.

How would his audience have felt? Chances are there would be at least two or three people counting the "uh's" they were hearing. Some of those in the back of the crowd would probably have had difficulty hearing parts of his speech because he may not have been breathing properly, which would cause his projection to trail off. Some would think he was speaking too fast as they would have had trouble processing what he was saying. Some would begin to question his knowledge level and confidence in the words he was saying. Which means many in his audience would not have heard these words, "... and that government of the people, by the people, for the people, shall not perish from the earth."

We know you have had similar reactions when you hear people speak and it sounds like rambling. And there may be times when people have had those reactions when you speak.

If you want to influence others to take action, you need for them to get the idea of what you are asking them to do. In order for that to happen most effectively, you need to pause. The lack of pauses is the number one habit we work with people to correct. Asking people to pause is also where we get the most initial resistance. And yet, at the end of our group workshops or individual consultations, pause is consistently the biggest "ah-ha" our participants experience.

Based on our experience with people's reactions, we know some of you are already thinking of why you would tell us you cannot pause. We have heard it all.

- "I only have a limited time with some of the people I talk to." No matter how much time you have, it is imperative you give them the time to digest what you have said. If you do not, it sounds like a verbal onslaught.

- "People will interrupt me if I pause." Most people interrupt when they have stopped listening to what someone is saying. All they are listening for is that moment when the speaker finally takes a breath. They will take that opportunity to interrupt.

- "People will think I do not know what I am talking about." Your audience can only know you are knowledgeable if you give them time to think.

- "I am afraid I will forget what I have to say." Here is the good news. Most people speak at an average of 125 words per minute. Most people think at an average of 500 words per minute. Your mind will work for you if you pause. We have had numerous instances when someone will get up to speak, say a word or two and then immediately say, "Can I start over?" We are always astounded because the person has not given themselves even a nanosecond to think of what they wanted to say. We capture many of these moments on DVD. What is great is when we play it back, the person always realizes he or she did not take any time to think.

- "I am afraid of the silence." We feel the fear of silence comes from the reasons for not pausing we just identified. When someone does not stop talking it can sound like white noise. That is not good. White noise lulls people to sleep. That is the silence you should really be afraid of.

As people practice pausing with us, the resistance fades fast because of the immediate benefits they realize.

What are the benefits to you when you pause?

- You can gather your thoughts and stay on track.

- You have time to breathe and relax.

- You can control your pace. We have many people tell us they think they speak too fast or others have told them that. We have only told a handful of people they speak too quickly. We have told thousands they just need to stop speaking. Pausing is not about speaking slowly. It is about breathing.

What are the benefits to your audience when you pause?

- They can process what you say. Remember most people think an average of 500 words per minute. They can quickly grasp what you say, but they can only do that when you pause.

- They are able to have a real image of what you are saying to them. Pauses give them the ability to relate their own experiences to what you are saying.

- It gives them time to formulate questions they may have.

- Pauses let them know you know your stuff.

How do you pause?

- Simply stop talking. Breathe.

- Eliminate the filler words. Here is what the segment of the Gettysburg Address we cited at the beginning would sound like without filler words: *"Four score and seven years ago, our fathers brought forth upon this continent a new nation: conceived in liberty, and dedicated to the proposition that all men are created equal. Now we are engaged in a great civil war testing whether that nation or any ..."*

    o The words that have been eliminated are: uh, you know, basically, actually, like, so, but. With the exception of "uh," all of these are real words, but they are meaningless when used simply to fill space.

- Think in terms of verbally punctuating your language. When you come to a comma, pause. When you come to a period, pause longer. When you come to a question mark, pause even longer.

- Pause for all the time that is needed. One second, two seconds, three seconds and occasionally even longer. You will know what is needed because, just like your audience, you now have time to think about what you are saying.

- Speak in shorter thoughts or sentences. This does not mean speak as though you are just learning to talk. Compare the sections of the Gettysburg Address that are in this segment. The one with the filler words ends up being one really long, unintelligible sentence. The one without fillers and real punctuation is two sentences that include sections divided with commas. It is easier to say and, as a result, easier to understand.

When should you pause?

- Any time you speak: face-to-face, at meetings or at group presentations.
- After you ask a question.
- When you want to emphasize a point or idea.
- When you need to take time to gather your thoughts.
- When you want or need to refer to your notes.
- When you move your eyes from one person to another.
- When you interact with PowerPoint or other visual aids.

The power of the pause is phenomenal. We consistently have individuals tell us how much control they have over their delivery and message when they pause. The power of the pause has been celebrated since at least the first century B.C. Publilius Syrus, a Latin writer of maxims, said, *"I have never regretted my silence, I have regretted my speech."*

POSTURE !

"Stand up straight."
– Everyone's mother

Have you ever been told to stand or sit up straight? We can still hear the sound of our mothers' voices today every time we slouch.

There are a variety of ways you can choose to stand or sit. These include crossing your arms, fidgeting with your rings or fingers, leaning off to one side, or placing your hands in your pockets, on your hips or behind your back. We are not saying this is wrong. We are saying these can give a different impression than you may want to convey to someone who sees you sitting or standing that way.

We ask groups to stand or sit in ways we have mentioned above and tell us their impressions of what they see. When people have their arms crossed, we hear "stand-offish," "closed" or "defensive". When they have hands behind their back, we hear "it looks like they are hiding something." When they sit or stand fiddling with their rings, fingers or pens, we hear "distracted" or "not interested". When they slouch whether sitting or standing, we hear "immature" or "too casual".

Make sure your posture does not sabotage your message. You can convey confidence the minute you walk into a room without saying a word. This confidence is portrayed with an open posture.

When you are standing, stand with your legs hip-width apart and your feet pointing forward. Allow gravity to do what it does best by relaxing your arms at your sides. If you are sitting down right now, take a moment to stand up and try this posture. Does it feel awkward or uncomfortable? If you are thinking yes, you are probably taking a step outside of your comfort zone because this is not how you usually stand. The good news is it can quickly become comfortable because you can practice it every time you stand.

Begin to use this open posture as your home base. It is the place to begin and always come back to when you are not moving or gesturing. It is a win for you and your audience. It conveys you are open and ready to have a conversation with them.

When you are sitting, similar techniques apply. Sit up straight with your feet flat on the floor and your hands resting comfortably on top of the table or desk. If there is not a table or desk in front of you, rest your arms on your lap or the arms of the chair.

Something as simple as having good posture will help you immediately connect with your audience. In addition, you will make your mother proud.

PRACTICE !

A few weeks ago a participant in our session asked us, "What tips would you share with me when I do not have time to practice?" Our response was simple: "We do not have any recommendations. You need to make the time to practice."

What do you not have time to practice? You can pause throughout the day when you are having a conversation. When you are standing or sitting you can practice using confident, open posture. When you are presenting or having a face-to-face conversation you can practice connecting with your eyes, and the list goes on and on. Reading this book is not enough if you want to be at your very best. If it was that easy, everyone would be effective communicators.

You have heard the quote, "practice makes perfect." We do not want you to think you need to be perfect. We are recommending you change this quote to "practice makes permanent." Imagine the amount of practice, determination and hard work required for a musician prior to playing in a symphony or for a dancer before performing in a theater in front of hundreds. These individuals are at their best because they are constantly practicing. They know the success of their performance is a result of practice. Because they are so skilled at what they do, often people will describe them as being natural. What those people lose sight of is someone who appears natural at something became that way because of the amount of practice they put into it.

What are you waiting for? Begin to **Practice** today.

Yes You Can!

PAUSE !

- Use the pause in EVERY conversation you have. Not just business related.

- For at least one month, review your voice mail messages before you send them out. Monitor the progress you make eliminating filler words and adding pauses.

- Write your filler word on a post-it note and place this note in front of you at your desk, at a meeting, etc. to remind you to pause.

- On occasion, audiotape yourself.

- Ask for feedback from family, friends and peers.

POSTURE !

- Pay attention today to your posture when you are standing or sitting. Remind yourself of the techniques under **Posture** every time you begin to slouch, lean or fidget.

- When you are standing talking to friends, family or co-workers, practice your new posture.

- Take a look at photos or videos to give yourself feedback on what your posture conveys.

PRACTICE !

- Take five minutes out of every morning, afternoon and evening to consciously practice a new behavior or skill.

Add any other ideas you have for yourself

_____

_____

_____

_____

_____

_____

QUESTIONS

You have just concluded an outstanding presentation, face-to-face conversation or a meeting and now dread the inevitable questions. For many, the most frightening part of any conversation is the unscripted part. What if someone asks you a question you cannot answer? What if the audience turns hostile? What if someone asks such a lengthy and complex question that it wipes your mind clear of all the knowledge stored in your brain? What if someone wants to make you look stupid?

These feelings can cause you to overlook the value of asking for questions from your audience. The questions they have can:

- Create participation
- Enhance relationships
- Enable you to provide clarification
- Help you prevent miscommunication
- Increase your knowledge

How you handle questions can strengthen or weaken your credibility you have worked so hard to establish. Here are some Do's and Don'ts to consider.

Do

- Communicate to your audience you are open and willing to take their questions. Avoid fidgeting, crossing your arms or slouching. Avoid stepping back or leaning away from your audience.

- Connect with a questioner's eyes when they ask a question. This shows you are listening.

- Let the questioner finish before beginning your answer. You increase your chances of providing the correct answer.

- If the question can be answered with a simple yes or no, say yes or no first before you give any explanation.

- If necessary, check for understanding by paraphrasing the question back to the questioner.

- Pause before you answer. This gives you time to think.

- When communicating to two or more individuals, begin by saying one or two sentences to the initial questioner. Then continue your answer to others, one sentence per audience member. This enables everyone to feel included.

- Be brief. Answer only what is asked. The more you talk, the greater you risk getting off track, not answering the question and losing the attention of your audience.

- Use acknowledgment when appropriate to let the questioner know they have been heard.

- When answering a hostile or negative question, link your answer to the audience's benefits. For example, let's say you are asked this question: "How can we possibly afford the time and money it will take to train our management staff on this new product?" Your answer might be, "I understand your concern with cost, especially since the company has been cutting costs for the past quarter. First, we will save you time and money by training your management staff for you. We have worked with a variety of industries similar to yours with proven immediate results. With our experience, your staff will learn practical methods to work efficiently with this product. Past clients have earned a return on their investment in as little as three months after the product training date."

- Admit when you do not know an answer and let the questioner know when you will get back to them. Be sure to make a note to yourself as a reminder and let them see you do this.

Don't

- Raise your voice or invade the questioner's space as you are answering a question.

- Say, "good question." People often use this phrase as a filler to buy them time to think of an answer. You run the risk of offending others that you do not recognize with this phrase.

- Repeat questions simply to buy you time to think of an answer. In a group setting, repeating a question can be helpful if you are concerned others did not hear the question.

In addition ask your audience questions. Your questions can help:

- Encourage participation

- Give your audience the opportunity to have a say in your message

- Communicate to your audience you are curious

- Provide you with information you have not heard before

- Show your audience you care about the information you are giving them

When you follow these Do's and Don'ts, you will maintain and strengthen the credibility and confidence you have worked so hard to achieve. You will be perceived as a sincere listener who invites interaction and acknowledges others' concerns.

Quotes

Always bear in mind your own resolution to succeed is more important than any one thing. Do not be too timid or squeamish about your actions. All life is an experiment. The more experiments you make, the better. The wisest mind has something yet to learn.

We agree with everything in that paragraph. The problem is those are not our words. The entire paragraph is made up of quotations from others. The first sentence, spoken by President Abraham Lincoln, would fit in very nicely with the section on **Attitude**. The three sentences following the Lincoln quote were spoken by George Santayana, philosopher (1863-1952). Under **Zero In** we ask you to commit to an action plan. His words capture the commitment we want you to make. The last sentence is a quote from Ralph Waldo Emerson, essayist (1803-1882). In that one sentence he summarizes what we said under **Knowledge**.

Quotes are easy to find. Research the Internet, read the paper, listen to others. There are many benefits to using quotes.

- They can enhance your credibility. Knowing your audience will help you decide what sources to use. You want to be sure you do not have to preface every quote with an explanation of whom you are quoting.

- They can add humor or insight to your message.

- They can help your audience remember a key point or concept.

- They can help you make your point quicker. Refer back to the simple quote we use to begin **Posture**. When we use that quote in our workshops, everyone immediately stands up straight.

Whom should you quote? Business leaders, political figures, movie stars, singers, authors or your Uncle Dan. Just about anyone as long as there is a link to the point you are making. Attribute the quote to the person who said it, and for an anonymous quote state the source as unknown.

Where can you use quotes? They can be used in your beginning statements to immediately grab attention. They can be used throughout your message. They can also be used in your ending statements to focus on the point you were making.

When you are writing, quotes stand out as they are enclosed in quotation marks. When you are speaking it is necessary to attribute the quote to someone before you state it. Here are some ways to do that.

- You can tie the quote to a relevant point. Thomas Mann, the German novelist, once said, "Thoughts come clearly while one walks."

- You can ask the audience a question. "Who said, I hear and I forget, I see and I remember, I do and I understand?" People may have a variety of guesses. You want to emphasize Confucius was credited with saying that more than 2,500 years ago. Then tie the quote to the point you want to make. In this case you may be delivering a message about adult learning.

- You can simply say, "Bill Gates once said …"

It is generally better to use short quotes. You can remember them easier, which means your audience can also. If you need to read a quote, do so. Let your audience know that is what you are doing.

There are some things to avoid when using quotes.

- Repeatedly using the same types of quotes, e.g., sports quotes, business quotes, movie quotes, etc.

- Using quotes from controversial figures.

- Being tentative about your reference.

You can use quotes in all circumstances: face-to-face conversations, meetings or presentations. Just as the French author Anatole France once said, *"When a thing has been said and well, have no scruple. Take it and copy it."* But remember to always give credit to the person who said it.

Yes You Can!

QUESTIONS

- Start thinking in advance about questions you may get from your audience so you are prepared for them. One option is to ask a peer who may have more experience on the topic or with this particular audience what questions you may expect.

- If there are questions you think you will get, consider including the answers to these questions in your message.

- Pay attention to how you answer questions from family, friends and co-workers. Do you tend to interrupt their questions? Does it take you too long to get to your point?

QUOTES

- If you usually do not use quotes, Google your subject to find a quote to add more impact to a key point or idea.

Add any other ideas you have for yourself

_____

_____

_____

_____

_____

_____

R

READING YOUR AUDIENCE !

Knowing what to look for will better prepare you to accurately read your audiences' non-verbal cues. Be careful of making assumptions too quickly based on only what you see.

We once misread one of our audience member's non-verbal cues. As we began the workshop with a group discussion about the day's agenda and expectations, one individual in particular stood out. He was leaning back in his chair with his arms crossed. Whenever we would look at him, he would quickly glance away. This continued throughout the morning. In addition, his neutral facial expression made him appear bored and even distracted at times.

We approached him during the first break and asked him his impressions of the workshop. He told us he had found the information practical and useful. He also told us the videotaping was eye-opening for him. We were stunned. What we thought we were seeing was so different from the reality. It was interesting as we observed him after he told us that, we could detect subtle cues that showed he was taking in what we said.

We continue to experience similar scenarios at times in our workshops. We know from experience people listen and learn in different ways. People can display some unusual facial expressions and posture as they listen and learn. We have learned to identify which non-verbal cues we need to pay attention to and what to do about them.

When do you need to do pay attention?

- When you see a definite shift in someone's behavior. You may have someone who constantly smiles and nods their head as you present information. Suddenly they seem to have a scowl and have begun to avoid your eyes when you look their way.

- When several individuals look concerned or confused.

- When several people start nodding off or looking at their watches.

What can you do?

- If you have concerns about an individual, have a conversation with the person during a break. Politely ask them how they feel the presentation, meeting or conversation is going. Until this conversation takes place, you should continue to include him or her with your eye contact.

- If several people look confused or concerned, ask if there are questions, concerns or thoughts anyone has.

- If several people begin to nod off or fidget, it may be time for a break.

It would be a perfect situation if every person you spoke to looked back at you with a smiling, friendly face. That is not reality. There is no need to panic or immediately intervene the next time you see a person with closed posture, leaning back in the chair, or hardly looking at you. It could simply be the way someone looks as they listen and learn.

Yes You Can!

READING YOUR AUDIENCE !

- Begin to realize you may not have 100% audience attention all the time. Only react when it is really necessary. Avoid reacting too quickly to non-verbal cues.

- To effectively read your audience you need to be paying attention to them. Refer back to the **Yes You Can!** section under **Eyes** for suggestions on becoming comfortable with eye contact.

- Be wise about your interventions.

Add any other ideas you have for yourself

_____

_____

_____

_____

_____

_____

SMART!

"If you aim at nothing, you'll hit it every time."

— Unknown

Are you familiar with the concept of **SMART** goals? These are goals that are specific, measureable, attainable, relevant and timely. They help you focus your efforts and give a clear definition of what needs to be done. If you really want to accomplish your goals, it requires more than just writing down action steps. Be **SMART** when writing your personal goals and when you are asking your audience to take action to ensure they are:

- Specific. State clearly what you want to accomplish in concrete terms that can be easily measured and understood. Ask yourself, what outcome do I expect? You are more likely to accomplish your goal when it is specific rather than general.

    o   General goal: "I am going to pause when I speak."

    o   Specific goal: "Tonight for five minutes at dinner I am going to ask my family to immediately bring to my attention when I do not pause and when I say "uh's" and "um's."

- Measurable. Allow for some form of reliable measurement. When you are able to measure your progress you will stay focused, stay on track, and stay motivated to reach your targeted time frame. You will feel a sense of accomplishment when you can measure your success, which will give you the drive to continue pushing forward.

Ask yourself how you will know when you have accomplished your goal.

- o Non-measurable goal: "I want to influence others to take action."

- o Measurable goal: "Before my department meeting this afternoon, I will prepare three action steps for my team to accomplish by next week's meeting."

- Attainable. Goals must be reasonable and attainable. Having high goals that stretch and challenge you is important. They also need to be realistic or you will never accomplish them. They must be neither too easy that they require no significant effort, nor so difficult they cannot be accomplished. Consider the following questions to check for reality in your ability to accomplish your goals.

  - o What is most important to me?

  - o Does the goal ask for too big or too little of an improvement?

  - o Does the goal ask for a great deal more or less than I have been able to accomplish in the past?

  - o Do I have the opportunity to achieve the goal in a realistic time frame?

When you take the time to ask yourself these questions and be realistic with yourself, you will develop attitudes, abilities and skills to accomplish your goals.

o   Unattainable goal: "Every meeting I facilitate will be effective."

o   Attainable goal: "Beginning with the next meeting I facilitate, I will prepare an agenda and follow it."

- Relevant. The goal must be relevant to what you want to accomplish and must contribute to your overall goal. You are more likely to succeed when your goals have a purpose and are a reflection of who you are and what is important to you. They must be relevant to how hard you are willing and able to work. They must be relevant based on the availability of resources, knowledge and time.

  o   Irrelevant goal: "Within one year I want to travel the world delivering seminars."

  o   Relevant goal: "Within two months I will develop and deliver a seminar on product knowledge for my team."

- Timely. The goal must have a clearly defined time frame. Without a specific date or time to accomplish your goal, there is no sense of urgency, which provides a breeding ground for procrastination.

  o   Untimely goal: "I am going to write action steps."

  o   Timely goal: "By the end of today I am going to write three action steps identifying how I will begin improving my communication skills immediately based on what I have read in this book."

Throughout this book we have been asking you to take on a new challenge, changing your communication behavior to influence others to take action. Identifying **SMART** goals is a critical step. In the next section we ask you to take more steps.

STEP OUTSIDE YOUR COMFORT ZONE !

What are your favorite comfort foods? Ours include banana pudding, mashed potatoes and gravy, warm double chocolate brownies and others that are high in calories. If you are like us, it usually feels great when you eat your favorite comfort foods. It probably does not feel so great when you have to work out extra hard for two hours due to the five minutes it took you to eat that second helping. You may even feel some guilt for not sticking to your promise to at least skip that second helping.

Eating comfort foods can work against you. Staying inside your comfort zone can also work against you. In order to be at your best, you have to push the walls of that zone outward.

Motivational speaker Jim Rohn has said, *"We must all suffer from one of two pains: the pain of discipline or the pain of regret. The difference is discipline weighs ounces while regret weighs tons."* Have there been times in your life you regret not having done something? There may be many reasons why you chose not to. Some of those reasons may have been perfectly legitimate at the time. Have there been times you chose not to try something simply because it felt uncomfortable? You chose instead to stay in your comfort zone. Any dictionary definition of the word comfort includes positive synonyms, such as "soothe, calm, reassure, ease, etc." We want you to look at the idea of comfort in a different way. Specifically, we want you to see that comfort is not always good for you.

It will not always be easy. When you eat comfort foods, the discomfort usually doesn't begin until after you are done eating. When you step outside of your comfort zone when trying new habits, the discomfort usually starts immediately. To be at your best, you need to step past that initial discomfort that is very often just disparity.

If you continue to push those walls of your comfort zone, you will soon feel more comfortable. We see this happen all of the time. We have heard groans and complaints when we ask people to try standing as described under **Posture**. We ask them to assume that posture at the beginning of every recording. After the third time or so, we will ask them how that posture feels. They always say it feels much better than it did originally. In order for them to get to that feeling, they had to continue to take steps out of their comfort zone.

Think about all the things you do well: drive, play golf, facilitate meetings or anything. The first time you tried these things you had to be uncomfortable. Something made you continue until you could do them without thinking about your discomfort.

This book is about being at your best. In order for you to be at your best, you have to keep taking steps. You cannot stand still. If you do, you will never achieve what you can. Our advice to you is to keep stepping.

SPONTANEITY!

One of the first things we ask people to do in some of our workshops is to introduce themselves to the other participants in a 90-second recorded exercise. We use this exercise to provide a baseline coaching on their delivery skills. Most people have a tendency to say "uh," slouch, fidget with their hands or exhibit other habits that may take away from how they would like to be perceived. We have a significant percentage of people tell us they never have those habits when they know what they are talking about. Really? Shouldn't they be experts about themselves?

We also do an exercise in which we ask people to practice their delivery skills talking about a topic we give them. The topics are always something people will have at least some awareness about: skydiving, walking a dog, making a pizza, painting a house, etc. We always tell them they can say anything they want. We just want them to really concentrate on the delivery skills. The first words we often hear are "I don't know anything about that topic," and they hem and haw until one of two things happens. We either prompt them with ideas or, more importantly, they pause to get their thoughts together. When that happens, they have something to say.

These exercises are examples of asking people to be spontaneous, to have the ability to think on their feet. We feel all of the angst people go through when they are asked to do this is based on the fear they are not prepared.

The good news is everyone has lots of experience with thinking on their feet. Studies say the majority of what we say is done without advanced preparation or thought. If you have had any conversations today, you have already had the opportunity to be spontaneous.

Something else that should help you think on your feet is to realize you are rarely, and most likely never, asked to speak about something you truly do not know anything about. In the first exercise described in this section, we ask people to introduce themselves. In the second exercise we ask them to speak about topics of which they have some awareness. One of the examples we mentioned is skydiving. Most people have not done this activity, but everyone knows something about it.

Do you still need reassurance it is okay to take the time you need to think on your feet? Consider this: People do not know what you are going to say. Until you say something, it is a mystery to them. You have the upper hand.

There are techniques that can help you be spontaneous.

- Express a point of view about a topic before you provide details. Let's say we just asked you to talk about skydiving. What is your first thought? If it is either, "I have never gone skydiving" or "I do not know anything about skydiving," it is hard to think what to say next. If you express a point of view such as, "I think you have to be crazy to skydive'" or "I would like to get up the nerve to try skydiving," it is easier to keep talking because there are reasons you have those thoughts.

- Prepare for some of the tough questions you may receive before a meeting, face-to-face conversation or presentation.

- Ask questions at times. If someone asks you to talk about a very broad subject, ask them what in particular they want you to concentrate on. If you are unsure why they are asking you something, ask them. By using clarifying questions, you can pare a broad or vague subject down to something manageable.

- Use the non-verbal skills you have already read about to help you be spontaneous.

    o Maintain an open posture. It keeps you centered and better able to put your thoughts together.

    o Pause and breathe. This helps you focus.

    o Use your eyes to connect with your audience. Remember, that connection also helps you focus your thoughts on what you need to say.

Why is the concept of spontaneity important to your ability to influence others? It is because you need to have the ability to act in the moment. You need to be able to think on your feet for the instances when you:

- Have prepared for a 30-minute presentation and are told, when you arrive, you only have fifteen minutes

- Are asked an unexpected question in a face-to-face conversation

- Have someone at a meeting raise a concern you had not considered

If you look back on our suggestions, you will see the best way to be spontaneous is to be prepared for it to happen.

Yes You Can!

SMART!

- Immediately after a presentation, meeting or face-to-face conversation, take five minutes to write down at least three action steps focusing on what you want to change and how you are going to accomplish this using the **SMART** technique.

- Go back and review what you have written after some time has passed. If you did not follow through on the action, is it possible any of the elements of **SMART** were missing?

- When you are influencing others to take action, encourage them to use the **SMART** technique.

STEP OUTSIDE YOUR COMFORT ZONE!

- Make a decision today to do something that is different from your day-to-day routine. Take a different route to work, eat something new, or ask for feedback. Push yourself! You may be surprised with the results.

SPONTANEITY!

- Occasionally ask your audience "What else do you need to know that I have not covered that is important to you?"

Add any other ideas you have for yourself

_____

_____

_____

_____

_____

_____

T

TIME

We have heard many people begin a conversation by saying, "I know you are busy so I won't take much of your time." We have heard others say during a presentation "I'll have to rush through this last part because I don't have a lot of time left." The irony is they are wasting the very thing they need, time.

Mick Jagger sings *"Time is on my side, yes it is."* We agree it is on your side, if you use it well. Here are some ideas that can help you do that.

MEETINGS

- Put a time limit on the meeting.

- Earn a reputation as one who begins and ends on time.

- Use the agenda to keep you on track.

- Send out pre-reading with specific instructions as to your expectations. It is important for everyone to be ready to discuss issues at the meeting.

- Arrive early to the meeting to ensure everything is in place.

- Refer to the additional ideas under **Meetings**.

FACE-TO-FACE CONVERSATIONS

- If you are having a conversation in your office, ensure you have arranged for any potential distractions to be put on hold.

- No matter where you meet, check in to be sure it is still a good time to have that discussion. If not, it may be best to reschedule.

- Arrive early if you are meeting someone to guarantee you will start on time as opposed to apologizing for being late.

PRESENTATIONS

- Practice the presentation before giving it. Use the 75% rule to time yourself. If you have been given twenty minutes, your last practice should come in at fifteen minutes. When you present to a live audience, there are things that can happen that will add to your time, which could throw you off. Based on the reaction you are receiving from your audience, you may decide to add additional information. Or you might receive more questions than anticipated during the presentation.

- If you were prepared to talk for twenty minutes but are told you only have ten minutes, avoid rushing through what you had originally planned to say. Instead, based on your audience's needs, decide which of your key points to focus on. When you organize your message, it is easier to make decisions about which key or sub-points to delete.

- Review your notes if you find yourself running out of time. Always remember you do not need to say everything you want to say. Say only what is critical for your audience. Do not sacrifice a strong ending.

- Arrive an hour ahead of time to set up. This also gives you time to meet and greet participants.

Whether you are in a meeting, having a face-to-face conversation or delivering a presentation and you are running out of time, pause to collect your thoughts. This will help you change your message on the fly without your audience being aware of it.

Your audience's impression of you begins the moment they see you. It continues until you say your last word. Have every moment be worth their time.

Yes You Can!

TIME

- If you have a tendency to arrive late, be the first to arrive this week.

- If you have a tendency to run over your allocated time, prepare for 25% less time than you have been given.

Add any other ideas you have for yourself

_____

_____

_____

_____

_____

_____

Unconscious Competence

We have asked you to step outside your comfort zone and try new ways of communicating when you are influencing others to take action. Whenever you learn any new skill you go through four stages of learning. These stages are represented in the following matrix:

Stage 1 **Unconscious Incompetence**	Stage 4 **Unconscious Competence**
Stage 2 **Conscious Incompetence**	Stage 3 **Conscious Competence**

While the originator of this concept is unknown, the benefits of understanding the stages have helped many. If you get nervous thinking about presenting to a group, the matrix offers some insight.

Think back to when you were a kid in the early stages of elementary school and had no fear of raising your hand and asking the teacher to "pick me, pick me" when she called for volunteers to speak in front of classmates. No matter how you performed, you probably received lots of praise. You were in the blissful stage of unconscious incompetence. You had no idea there were skills associated with presenting to a group.

Now skip forward to high school. You take a public speaking class. You have a well-intentioned teacher tell you to look over the heads of people you are speaking to if you feel nervous. You follow that advice. When you finally sneak a peek at your audience, you see half of the audience is not paying any attention. The other half has a look of utter boredom on their faces. You have quickly become aware of how deficient you may be in the skills associated with presenting to a group. You are now at the realistic stage of conscious incompetence. This stage can be so uncomfortable many people do not ever want to present to a group again.

We know that is not true for you. You bought this book. You are ready to move to the next stage. If you practice the suggestions in this book, you will be a confident, competent speaker very quickly. The skills may not seem comfortable at first. They take work. This is the conscious competence stage. If you are not used to standing tall with your hands at your side as we suggested under **Posture**, your arms will feel heavy and you will feel awkward. Remember what you read under **Disparity**. We guarantee no one else is even giving it a thought. It takes work to change habits.

We discuss the concept of reaching the unconscious competence stage in the workshops we conduct. It quickly becomes more than just theory. Participants see it come to life with the playbacks of their recordings. Almost everyone has habits they were unaware of. As they work to change those habits they see the work it takes becomes easier each time they practice.

It is worth the work. We remember a young woman who told us the concept reminded her of when she took up the sport of snowboarding. She was an excellent skier and assumed snowboarding would be easy. She said she was surprised and frustrated at first with how difficult it was. She wanted to quit but friends encouraged her to keep at it. She practiced one entire weekend and by the end was comfortable with her new sport. She said the next time she went snowboarding it was effortless. She said she would continue to think of this snowboarding experience whenever she felt uncomfortable trying a new habit with her communication skills.

With practice, you will develop new habits. These new habits can quickly become second nature to you. When that happens, you are at the unconscious competence stage.

Yes You Can!

UNCONSCIOUS COMPETENCE

- Think about something you learned that was difficult at first. You may have had thoughts of giving up. You were possibly in Stage 2 or 3 of the unconscious competence matrix. Because you stuck with it, you are now glad you did.

- Now apply this concept to your face-to-face communication. If you begin to struggle at Stage 2 or 3, reflect back on a situation when you were determined to push through. Put this image of your earlier success in your mind to help you get through any new struggle.

Add any other ideas you have for yourself

_____

_____

_____

_____

_____

_____

Visual Aids

One of us sees a doctor who has terrific doctor-patient relationships. He always makes his patients feel in their short visits with him that he is only thinking about them. He is kind, has a great sense of humor and is passionate about his practice. He was asked to speak at a health-care luncheon about recent advances in the fight against a particular disease. His audience was going to be patients and their family members. We were invited to see him speak.

When we walked in, we saw he had a PowerPoint slide of a café in Italy displayed on a screen. We knew he had recently returned from a vacation there. We assumed his beginning statement was going to include a story that had a tie-in to quality of life. After he was introduced to the audience, he walked up to his computer, immediately went to the next slide that was filled with text of difficult medical terms and started talking to the screen. For the next twenty minutes, he showed us a deck of about thirty slides that might have had relevancy to an audience of doctors but had little, if any, relevancy to his current audience.

We saw him completely lose his personality. As a result, we saw an audience that lost interest very quickly.

Many presenters have forgotten the purpose behind visual aids. They seem to have forgotten what is more important, the visual aid or the audience. It often appears presenters use their visual aids to hide from their audiences. Often the presenters use their visual aids as their script. Visual aids have one purpose: to support your message. When we refer to visual aids in this section, we are referring to marketing pieces, props, flipcharts and PowerPoint slides. They are what you use as you are delivering your message. We are not referring to handouts, which are generally for your audience to take away with them for future reference.

When used appropriately, visual aids provide impact, control and emphasis for you, the audience and your message. According to a study by the University of Minnesota, visual aids increase your chance of persuading your audience to accept your position by 43%. In addition, studies by Harvard and Columbia show visual aids improve retention by up to 38%.

We are going to address using visual aids from two standpoints: their design and your interaction with them.

DESIGN

Whether you design visual aids yourself or use visual aids designed by others, keep the following in mind.

- What are the critical points you want your audience to remember? When you want to add emphasis and increase the chance your audience remembers a particular point, use a visual aid to help make the point.

- Less is more. Think about billboards or signs that grab your attention. We would guess these visual aids grab your attention because you can grasp the idea quickly. They are bold and brief.

- Determine which types of visual aids best support your message.

    o   Use flipcharts for smaller groups to encourage group discussions.

    o   Use props to demonstrate or show a new product.

o   Use PowerPoint to emphasize key points and graphs or
to illustrate photographs.

o   Use marketing pieces to emphasize key points about
your organization, products or services.

INTERACTION

Once the visual aids are designed, how you interact with them
will positively or negatively impact the amount of information your
audience remembers. We often ask participants in our workshop if
there is anything they dislike about the way others interact with visual
aids. The number one complaint is people talk to their visual aids and
not to their audience. The following can help ensure this is something
you never do. These skills apply to all visual aids during a presentation,
face-to-face conversation or a meeting.

- Pause immediately after displaying the visual aid to give yourself
time to think and to give the audience time to see, absorb and
understand.

- Pause and think about what you want to say every time you
look at the visual aid to gather your thoughts.

- Talk to the audience, not the visual aid. Turn from the visual
aid to the audience in silence, connect with their eyes and then
speak.

- Avoid fidgeting with your notes, marker, remote control, etc.
This behavior creates distractions.

- Remove the visual aid if it no longer supports your message.
For example, if you are explaining an idea while referring to a
marketing piece and you have now transitioned to a new subject,
place this piece off to the side. If you are using PowerPoint and

are not ready to go to the next slide, press the "B" key. This will blank the screen. Pressing "B" again brings it back.

- When you are using props such as a product, allow your audience to see and touch it before you talk about it. This approach works best when your audience is a small group. For larger groups, show the product in silence to give your audience a chance to see it. Then offer to have the product available to them after you are done talking.

Become familiar with your visual aids and how to work with them smoothly and effectively. Your knowledge of these resources is just as important as the knowledge you convey in relaying your message.

The next time you are having a face-to-face conversation, participating in a meeting or delivering a message, pay attention to how you interact with your visual aids. As is often said, "Seeing is believing." Good visual aid design and interaction can help your audience see key points you are making. It is also important your audience hears the points you are making.

VOCAL PROJECTION

A woman once told us someone at her organization said he always spoke at a low volume level in order to make people really pay attention to what he was saying. She asked what we thought of that idea. We asked her if it was effective at the meetings she attended when he spoke. She said it was not and in fact, others nicknamed the man the low talker. For anyone who is a Seinfeld addict, you will recognize that nickname from a memorable episode. If you have not seen that episode, believe us when we say speaking softly is not a way to get the attention or the action you want from others.

Vocal projection has nothing to do with yelling. It is the realization you need to use different volume levels so your voice reaches everyone in the room. No one should have to strain to hear you.

After we record people, we play their DVD's back for them. We put the volume at a set level. The level is one that lets us know if their volume levels are where they should be for the size of the group they are speaking to. If we have to turn it up to clearly hear what they are saying, that tells us we need to let them know they should be speaking at a higher level.

If we have to turn it up slightly, we may notice that as people are speaking they are holding their arms behind their back. We let them know by simply relaxing their arms, as we suggest under **Posture,** their volume will automatically increase.

If we have to turn the volume up significantly, we will ask the person to speak to us in increasing volume levels. We focus on three main ones. The level of volume they would use speaking to us face-to-face, the volume they would use if they were seated at a table speaking to five or six people, and the volume they would use if they were standing and speaking to a group of fifteen. All three of these levels should be easily within someone's capabilities, and all of them should feel comfortable.

We often hear people tell us they feel they are yelling when they practice the last level, and sometimes even the last two levels. If we are working with a group of people, we will ask the person we are coaching to practice projecting at higher levels in front of the others. We ask how the person sounds, and these are the types of words we always hear from the group: confident, passionate, enthused, energetic and so on. We have never heard the word loud, even though the person speaking at a higher level may feel he or she is yelling. Then we capture it on camera and let the person hear what the others heard. Without exception, the person becomes a believer in the power of vocal projection.

You will always sound louder to yourself than to others. When you hear yourself speak, you hear the sound resonate in your head. After all, you are closer to the source.

We have heard a number of reasons why some people have difficulty projecting their voices.

- Some people say it is part of their culture to speak softly. We ask them who the audiences are that they speak to. As businesses become more diverse and global, it is imperative the volume they use is appropriate for the audience they are speaking to.

- Some tell us they were raised to speak softly. We had one person tell us every time he spoke, he could hear his mother telling him to use his inside voice. Unfortunately, he had taken that to such an extreme no one outside of about five feet from him could hear him. We want everyone to still imagine your mother telling you to "stand up straight," but go ahead and ignore any inside voice comments.

- One man who was about 6'5" tall and weighed around 280 pounds told us he spoke softly because he was afraid of overpowering his audience. When we had him practice the third level of volume, he received the same comments others received: confident, passionate, enthused, energetic and so on. In his case, the word overpowering was never used.

- We have had others say they speak softly if they feel intimidated by someone in the room. Great.

If you want to influence others to take action they have to hear you. At the same time they do not want to feel they are being yelled at. In all of our years working with thousands of people, we can count on one hand the number of times we have had to turn the volume down as we were listening to the recording because someone was too loud.

We once had someone write on our evaluation that one of us had said something she would remember the rest of her life. She did not mention what it was. We have to assume whatever it was, it was something we said loud and clear. We also hope she wrote it down so she will truly remember it. The information under **Write it Down** tells you why we say that.

Yes You Can!

VISUAL AIDS

- Review a past or current PowerPoint presentation you will be using. How would you recreate these PowerPoint slides?

- For every visual aid you have, ask this question: "What is the key take away for your audience and does the design support your message?"

- Ask yourself why you are using a particular type of visual aid. Is this the best choice to support your message?

- Practice interacting with your visual aid in front of a mirror. Place your visual aid behind you and pretend your audience is the mirror. Only speak when you see yourself in the mirror to avoid talking to your visual aid.

VOCAL PROJECTION

- Practice sitting at your desk with an open posture. If you cross your arms in front of you or if you slouch in your chair, your voice gets lost.

- Audiotape your conversations to give yourself feedback on what your audience hears rather than what you hear. Experiment with different volume levels for face-to-face conversations, small groups and large group presentations. Your projection should be different each time.

Add any other ideas you have for yourself

_____

_____

_____

_____

_____

_____

WRITE IT DOWN

We learned a valuable lesson the first day we sat down to write this book. It was that at least one of us had to be capturing our thoughts as we brainstormed. Before we did that, we were constantly saying, "That's a great idea." Then two minutes later neither one of us could remember what we had said. We quickly got our laptops out and solved that problem by using the electronic version of writing it down.

People are often surprised at how short term their memories are. We think one reason is so much enters our minds. It is often hard for any one thing to have the impact it needs to.

There are a number of reasons to write things down.

- It will ensure your good ideas do not get lost.

- It will help you come up with other ideas. Think of it as your own personal brainstorming opportunity.

- It can help relieve stress at times. We sometimes feel over-whelmed with how much we have to do. We find if we write a to-do list of what needs to be done, it helps focus our minds on action rather than stress.

You can capture ideas on your laptop, in a journal, or in the memory function of your Blackberry or other technology. Writing things down can help you be at your best with many of the ideas we offer in this book.

- **Beginnings**, **Endings**, **Stories**, and **Quotes**. If you hear or read something that makes you think, laugh, or consider a different point of view, write it down. There is a chance it will make others have the same reaction you had. We saw this quote from Lily Tomlin recently: *"The road to success is always under construction."* The immediate thought was it was perfect for the book. If we had not written it down, it would have been forgotten.

- **Meetings**. Writing things down helps everyone focus. Use flipcharts to capture the agenda, ground rules or action items that are pertinent to the meeting. If items come up that are not on the agenda, write them down for future meetings.

- **Notes**. Write words or phrases on your notes that will prompt your memory if needed.

- **Objectives**. As we stated before, it is always important to know where you are going. The first thing we wrote for this book was the summary statement for the back cover. Whenever we found ourselves going off track, we would refer to what we had written.

  We once heard someone say he had a major life objective he wanted to accomplish. He wrote it on his bedroom ceiling so it would be the first thing he saw each morning when he would wake up. He met his objective. This may be extreme. We are not asking you to do that. We are asking you to put objectives in writing in some form.

- **Questions**. When people ask you a question and you tell them you need to get back to them later with the answer, write it down so you will remember it. When you do this, it is also a reassurance to the questioner you will remember to do so. We ask people if they like it when a waiter or waitress takes their order in a restaurant and does not write it down. Most people want to see a visual of someone writing the order down.

- **Zero In**. The last section in this book is your action plan. The first thing we do is include a quote that talks about the importance of having a pencil and paper to help you focus.

We asked you in the beginning of this book to make notes and to underline content that grabbed your attention. If you did this, take a look and write your notes down where you can have easy access to them.

Yes You Can!

WRITE IT DOWN

- Read this section again. It is all there for you.

Add any other ideas you have for yourself

_____

_____

_____

_____

_____

_____

X Marks the Spot

Any good treasure map would always have an X to mark the spot where the treasure was. Having that X did not mean it was necessarily easy to find the treasure. Can you imagine a pirate tale or an Indiana Jones movie where the hero finds the map and says, "Oh, I think the treasure is over there," digs for about two minutes and walks away with the treasure, knowing life will be forever at its best? We know for sure if that was all there was to it, there would not be the fourth movie of the Indiana Jones saga.

Finding the treasure always takes work, often results in some missteps along the way, but ultimately is worth the effort. We began this book by stating most of you can point to some success in your life when you were at your best while communicating. Not just good or adequate, but at your best. Being at your best should be the treasure you strive for.

We have given you a good start by providing you with practical suggestions under the **Yes You Can!** sections of the previous letters. You have now reached the spot where you decide what you are going to do with this information.

The remainder of this book under **Yes You Can!** and **Zero In** provide you with the final pieces of the map to help you dig deeper to continually reach that pinnacle of success.

Yes You Can !

We assume if you have made it this far you are excited about knowing that **Yes You Can!** be at your best when influencing others. You are not quite there yet. There is one more essential idea to take you from where you are now to where you need to be.

Making this change includes four steps: awareness, understanding, acceptance and taking action. These steps are often used by others to explain the four stages of organizational change. There is relevance to applying these four stages to yourself as you make changes to your habits.

Awareness

A pre-requisite for making a change is you are aware of your strengths, weaknesses and impact on others. In reading this book, you may have become aware of things you did not realize. To truly be aware you need to ask others to give you constructive feedback to be at your best. As long as we have been practicing in this industry we continue to work with coaches to help us reach our best. The biggest benefit we receive from our coaches is the awareness we experience on a daily basis.

A coach will help you realize there is something you can learn about yourself. What you become aware of might be unexpected and surprising, but that is the nature of making a change.

Understanding

This is the stage where the light bulb goes on and you say, "Ah ha!

I understand what needs to be done to make the change I want to make." If you are working with a coach, they will know when you reach understanding because they will see the light bulb go on. There are numerous occasions when we have seen this happen for individuals and we bet you have seen it too. Their eyes light up, their voice has excitement and their entire body language communicates they are now open and ready to move forward. They have reached a stage where they stop denying this change is needed and they are willing to accept it.

ACCEPTANCE

During this stage, you accept this can be the new you. You are more open-minded, and are now more interested in making the change. You are focused to move forward.

When you are in the acceptance stage you may be tempted to say, "Being okay is good enough. I don't always need to be at my best." Making changes will not be easy. This is another benefit to working with a coach. Your coach should be someone who can give you encouragement, direction and the push you need to keep you moving forward and taking action.

TAKING ACTION

Taking action is the most difficult step. What distinguishes a great communicator from an average communicator is this: Great communicators do what average communicators do not want to do. It would be easy to set this book next to the others on your bookshelf when you are done reading it and simply go on with your day-to-day, comfortable routine. We know you are not going to take the easy way out. You will actually take action today. Not tomorrow, not next week, but today to begin making changes so every essential idea in this book is now part of your modus operandi.

Zero In

"When you write down your ideas you automatically focus your full attention on them. Few if any of us can write one thought and think another at the same time. Thus a pencil and paper make excellent concentration tools."

– Michael Lebouef, author

We asked you to mark this book as you read it. We hope as you page back through the book you see comments you have made that will help you focus on what to do next to help you be at your best.

We firmly believe you can do everything you wish to. We also know you cannot do it all at once. Where do you start?

There are different ways to make that decision. We used the ! symbol to mark the items we felt were essential in all of your interactions when you want to influence others to take action. You may want to concentrate on the **Yes You Can!** suggestions within those items first. If you are going to present tomorrow using PowerPoint, concentrate today on the tips we suggest under **Visual Aids** even though that does not have the ! symbol.

You may want to put what you identified into natural groupings. For instance:

Content	Delivery Skills	Interaction with Audience	You
Beginnings	Body Language !	Audience !	Attitude !
Endings	Eyes !	Benefits	Authenticity !
Get to the Point	Facial Expressions	Disasters	Change
Humor	Gestures	Knowledge !	Confidence !
Introductions	Inflection	Lectern	Consistency !
Knowledge !	Movement	Listening !	Disparity
Notes	Pause !	Meetings	Expectations
Once Upon a Time	Posture !	Objective !	Fear
Organize !	Vocal Projection	Questions	Feedback !
Quotes		Reading Your	Habits
Time		Audience !	Integrity !
Write it Down		Visual Aids	Journey
			Kids
			Nervousness
			Opportunities !
			Practice !
			SMART !
			Spontaneity !
			Step Outside Your Comfort Zone !
			Unconscious Competence
			X Marks the Spot
			Yes You Can !
			Zero In

Within the groupings, there are items that have a definite effect on other items. For instance, if you work on items under **Disparity**, they can help increase your **Confidence.** If you decide to work on **Posture** for the next three weeks, **Gestures** will come easier to you. It will also be easier to use strong **Vocal Projection.** If you work on developing a memorable **Beginning** for your next presentation, it will be easier to have a powerful **Ending** as these two items share common elements. If you have a wealth of **Knowledge** about your **Audience**, it is much easier to know the types of **Questions** they may ask.

You will be changing some **Habits**. As we stated previously, it can take anywhere from seventeen to twenty-one days to break a habit. You will be **Stepping Out of Your Comfort Zone** quite a bit. We have one more suggestion. Do not take this on by yourself. Find others to give you **Feedback**.

We assume you are having some thoughts about what your next steps will be. We invite you to once again pick up a pen or pencil and start to **Write it Down** and organize those thoughts you are having on the two pages following this one.

ZZZZZZZ

Always get a good night's sleep. It is one of the best things you can do to be at your best and influence others to take action. Sweet dreams!

Write Your Thoughts Down

Write Your Thoughts Down

Postscript

As you read under **Journey**, being at your best is a continuous process. It takes time and work. Revisit this page after thirty days and ask yourself:

- How have you changed?

- What other changes do you want to make?

- What changes are you still resisting?

- What has been easier than you had expected?

- What has been more difficult than you had expected?

Keep coming back to this page every thirty days and your responses should be different if you are truly on a journey to be at your best.

LaVergne, TN USA
29 October 2010

202773LV00002B/2/P